TRUMP

THE BEST **REAL ESTATE ADVICE**
I EVER RECEIVED

D0954647

TRUMP

THE BEST REAL ESTATE ADVICE
I EVER RECEIVED

100 TOP EXPERTS SHARE THEIR STRATEGIES

DONALD J. TRUMP

THOMAS NELSON
Since 1798

NASHVILLE   DALLAS   MEXICO CITY   RIO DE JANEIRO

© 2006 by Donald J. Trump

All rights reserved. No portion of this book may be reproduced, stored in a retrieval system, or transmitted in any form or by any means—electronic, mechanical, photocopy, recording, scanning, or other—except for brief quotations in critical reviews or articles, without the prior written permission of the publisher.

Published in Nashville, Tennessee, by Thomas Nelson. Thomas Nelson is a registered trademark of Thomas Nelson, Inc.

Thomas Nelson, Inc., titles may be purchased in bulk for educational, business, fund-raising, or sales promotional use. For information, please e-mail SpecialMarkets@ThomasNelson.com.

ISBN 978-1-4016-0530-8 (TP)

Library of Congress Cataloging-in-Publication Data

Trump, Donald, 1946-
    Trump: The Best Real Estate Advice I Ever Received / Donald J. Trump.
        p.cm.
Includes index.
        ISBN 978-1-4016-0255-0 (hard cover)
        1. Real estate investment I. Title.
        HD1382.5.T78 2006
        332.63'24—dc22

                                                            2006021520

Printed in the United States of America

QG D2-19-16

CONTENTS

CONTENTS

CONTENTS

CONTENTS

CONTENTS

CONTENTS

CONTENTS

CONTENTS

INTRODUCTION

I've wanted to write this book for years.

Anyone who's observed my career is aware of my real estate strategies. (And if you haven't observed my career, now is the time to watch me on television or pick up one of my previous books.)

While very successful, my real estate business doesn't cover everything that's happening in real estate. What I know, I know well, but I don't have a monopoly on good ideas and real estate wisdom. I can't know everything. As Susan Penzer points out, underlying my success is my "ability to gather the best information from the brightest people." Susan made that comment after watching how I did business. But that's also exactly what I've done in this book—gather the best information from the brightest people in real estate. They share their experience, the lessons they've learned from others, and the lessons they've learned from the mistakes they have made and almost made. *The Best Real Estate Advice I Ever Received* is sage wisdom garnered from one hundred leaders in the field of real estate—the kind of information and wisdom that you can get only from a lifetime of experience.

In this book you'll find tremendous insight based on positive experience and lessons learned the hard way by real estate moguls from around the country. From missed opportunities, to wrong guessing about the market, to under or over negotiating—there are a lot of ways all of us could have done it better. These men and women tell you what they have learned.

I am friends with some of these contributors and some I've never met, although I've admired them from afar. This book represents the best compendium of real estate advice ever assembled. And I think that it accomplishes its mission: to offer you help in planning your own success in real estate. Whether it's buying or selling your own house, condo, or co-op, or whether you're in or entering the real estate business, I think you'll learn a lot from *The Best Real Estate Advice I Ever Received*.

BUY WHERE THE WEALTHY LIKE TO PLAY

ARTHUR L. ALLEN

Arthur L. Allen is founder, president, and
CEO of Allen Systems Group, Inc. (ASG).

Computer software has been my focus, my passion, and
my life since I began working as a systems analyst
nearly forty years ago. But one of my most profitable decisions, and one in which I take great satisfaction today, is my
decision to act on a friend's real estate advice.

Regardless of downturns in the economy or slumps in
the technology markets, my real estate investments in
Naples, Florida, have flourished. I will always be grateful
that I acted on my friend's advice, and kept investing over
the years. If I were to generalize about this real estate
advice and why it turned out to be so successful, I would
say, buy real estate where the wealthy like to play.

When I moved to Naples in the seventies, this Gulf
Coast community in southwest Florida was already a

popular winter-residence community for many of the country's most affluent families. I certainly recognized the importance of Naples's climate, and few places matched its natural beauty. I did not think much about real estate investments, however, until my friend gave me this advice: "Buy all the real estate you can in Naples. It's a unique place, and you will make a lot of money investing in property here." At that time I started thinking about Naples real estate in other ways than just being a great location for my software company.

I knew the history of this part of Florida and that it attracted many wealthy people. Some of its early residents included such notable figures as Thomas Edison, Henry Ford, Harvey Firestone, Greta Garbo, Gary Cooper, and Barron G. Collier.

In the fall of 1975 I bought my first home in Naples, and I have been buying and selling real estate here since then. I have made many millions by following this advice. I paid $875,000 for that first property, and it is now valued at well over $14 million.

Even though my business now has fifty offices worldwide, I still have my company headquarters in Naples, Florida. Naples has grown many times over since I bought my first property, and it still attracts affluent individuals escaping from the cold winters of the North. People come here for many reasons—to play golf or tennis, to enjoy their pleasure yachts, and to retire. More than two hundred current or former Fortune 500 CEOs have homes here, as well as such celebrities as Larry Bird, Mike Ditka, Greg Norman, Mary Carillo, and many, many others.

DON'T BE AFRAID TO INVEST TIME

ADINA AZARIAN

Adina Azarian is president and CEO of Adina Real Estate
and a member of the Real Estate Board of New York.

Real estate is all about wasting time. The more time you waste, the more money you make.

If you are a person who thinks about conserving your time, then you are not right for the real estate business, or you need to change your thinking. When I first started in the real estate business, I felt I was wasting a lot of my time—whether it was making phone calls to find listings or working with clients that I wasn't able to close. After some time, I went to my trainer and said, "I feel that I am wasting a lot of my time."

And he said, "Real estate is all about wasting time. The more time you waste, the more money you make." So instead of giving up, I kept at it, and things started to click. Eventually phone calls turned into listings, and appointments with clients turned into closings. The more and more I did it—even though, sure, sometimes things didn't work out—technically, the more time I spent at least making the effort, the better the results.

Cutting back—saying, "I won't meet as many clients today," or "I won't make as many phone calls today"—doesn't work in the real estate business. You must never view any time you spend working as a waste of time in order to become very successful in real estate. The more people you put yourself in front of, the more phone calls you make, or the more doors you knock on, the more money you will make. It's simple. So whenever one of my salespersons comes to me and says, "I wasted so much time with that client and I didn't close," or something to that effect, I remind her that the closings will come with time and experience and she simply can't gain experience without wasting her time! And don't forget to send a thank-you card, even to those clients you didn't close. Now that's the right thinking!

BUY THE BEST

ROGER BARNETT

Roger Barnett is chairman and CEO of Shaklee Corporation,
a natural nutrition company, and founder of Beauty.com.

Buy the best. The best will always retain its value and appreciate at a faster rate. The best is always expensive today, but is always a good value tomorrow.

I purchased a building in New York City that was run by a foundation. At the time, it was one of the higher-priced single-use sales in the city. However, with the great structure, desirable location, and unusual width and proportions, I invested in bringing it to state of the art. Today it is worth three times my total cost, which is a significantly higher return than that from the rest of the real estate market.

FOCUS ON RESULTS

4

THOMAS J. BARRACK JR.
Thomas J. Barrack is chairman and CEO of Colony Capital,
a private international real estate investment firm.

D on't confuse efforts with results.

LISTEN TO YOUR 5 CLIENT'S NEEDS

MONDA BASSIL

Monda Bassil is president of Prestigious Properties of New York.

The best real estate advice I ever received was to listen to my client's needs. It's something I do each and every day. A truly successful real estate professional should know: (1) the client's needs and lifestyle; (2) the neighborhoods he or she is marketing; and (3) current market conditions.

You must prepare well for every appointment and do your homework, earnestly and methodically. If your Tuesday morning appointment mentions that he is a gourmet cook, you must know the available houses well enough to focus only on those properties that will fit his needs. Get organized, do your research, and don't bother showing him a loft with an under-equipped galley kitchen, no matter how stunning it is. If your latest referral is a couple who is downsizing, listen when they tell you about their lifestyle and interests. Does the property have a garden? Is the theater nearby? Is there enough space for grandchildren to visit?

In residential sales especially, service means a full understanding of areas, markets, and most important, people. I often say, "We don't sell, we educate." It is crucial, though, to read "educate" not as if we are teaching clients, but listening to clients. Your clients are entrusting their home search to you, and you must utilize the entire marketplace to find a great fit. You must also understand the neighborhoods you are marketing in order to match the neighborhood to the buyer's personality. Ask yourself, What kind of opportunities does this neighborhood offer to the buyer?

You know the desired product, you know the neighborhood, and you know the market, but you cannot sell any one of those as a separate entity. Instead all three must combine correctly to give your client a safe haven. This home is where your clients will open their eyes the first thing in the morning and turn off the lights at night. They need to feel a sense of comfort. You are guiding them in the most important purchase of their lives, the one that involves the largest percentage of every dollar earned. You must find the perfect match for your client's needs and the available property in their desired neighborhood. It's not easy, but with hard work and perseverance, it is very rewarding when that right match happens.

In some ways, real estate is like the theater. You read the script, you rehearse, you rehearse even more, and then it's showtime. You are patient; you recognize that a perfect performance takes an enormous amount of preparation and lots of time; and you know you can't go wrong if you study and prepare. Also, you admit that part-time isn't good enough. If you say, "I'm keeping my other job, just in case this doesn't work," you can bet it won't.

Once you understand that you are selling a safe haven by matching up your client with the right neighborhood in the right market and spend the time and effort to make this your career, be it in investment where the excitement is, in development, or in sales, you just might learn the great secret: real estate can be so much fun you almost feel guilty earning money at it!

TARGET GROWTH AREAS, AND TRY NOT TO SELL WHAT YOU OWN

DOUGLAS BAUMWALL

Douglas Baumwall is a certified business intermediary
with Collins & Collins Investments whose articles have been
published by the Florida Association of Realtors and
Florida Commercial magazine.

I received two pieces of advice that may be of interest to real estate investors.

The first is to target an area outside a city in the direction of growth. Then shop for raw land on a primary artery where you may purchase by the acre instead of by frontage.

The second is to try not to sell your own real estate unless it's too small to be managed efficiently. It can be a good idea to purchase real estate, and it can be a good idea to sell other people's real estate (either by flipping a purchase contract prior to closing or by owning a brokerage company).

11

WORK WITH PROFESSIONALS YOU TRUST

JOHN BEARDEN

John Bearden is president and CEO of GMAC Home Services.
Koenig & Strey GMAC Real Estate, a GMAC entity, was
selected to exclusively market the Trump International
Hotel and Tower in Chicago.

My best real estate advice sounds simple, and that's because it is. But don't let its simplicity obscure how important it is.

Find a real estate professional you can trust.

I mean, *really* trust.

For many people, buying or selling a home is one of the single largest investments (and accompanying financial transaction) they'll ever make. Believe me, you do not want to hand this very important—and extremely complex—process to someone you don't trust completely, and who may not have your best interests at heart.

Like so many people, my wife and I learned this hard-knocks lesson long ago through firsthand experience.

We've bought and sold several homes through the years, and we've lost money on only one of them . . . *our very first home*. Why? Because we didn't realize then, as we do now, how wise it is to take the time to find a real estate professional who knows what he is doing; whose passion for the job shines through in genuine concern for, and the desire to help, his customers.

Unfortunately the agent we chose (rather quickly and without a whole lot of research on our part) gave us bum advice. The only thing worse than her advice was her communication, which was pretty much nonexistent. I'll never forget what she told us—"I'll let you know when the closing date is"—because I now understand what she was really telling us: "I'll let you know when my commission check is ready." She might just as well have added: "Until then, don't bother me."

So, my bottom line is, find someone you can trust. Take your time and search for someone with whom you can build a mutually beneficial, long-term relationship; someone whose full-time career is real estate—not your friend's uncle who closes two transactions every three years. Look for someone who values a relationship more than a commission from a single transaction. Get opinions from friends and neighbors: Who did they use and why? Will they use that agent again when they buy or sell a home? Once you find that "someone special," hang on to him or her through the years as your trusted adviser and skilled negotiator.

Good agents pledge up front to make you partners in the process and to act as your trusted adviser. They spell out for you—figuratively and in some cases literally—what they'll do for you and when they'll do it and why. And after they're done, they ask for your honest feedback. They know the ins and outs of their market—*your* market—including anything and everything about the neighborhood and community (types of homes, the quality of local schools, nearby parks, and so on) that will help you make not just an informed decision, but the right decision.

So there it is—the best real estate advice I have to offer. I hope it not only helps you avoid the problems that can so easily sidetrack home buyers and sellers, but it actually makes the process what it truly should be: a wonderful, exciting, and life-changing experience.

ALWAYS DO THE VERY BEST YOU CAN

FRANK G. BINSWANGER JR.

Frank G. Binswanger is chairman of Binswanger, a family-owned
international real estate leader with 160 offices worldwide.

Our father, who started the Binswanger company in the middle of the Depression, always told us, "Never try to burn the candle at both ends." You are either a broker or an investor/developer. You are representing a client, or you are representing yourself. In the simplest terms, you cannot honestly serve two masters. Although such advice is controversial in today's environment, it was a sound business decision at the time, and our business has thrived as our company was able to devote our full attention to representing the client without conflict.

It was evident in the 1960s and 1970s that corporations and institutions wanted a single source to handle their real estate needs in the U.S. and across the globe. As a result, expansion from a regional firm to a national and ultimately international organization was an obvious course for us to follow. In addition, the company's operating disciplines were expanded to provide financial services, property and project management, appraisal, and strategic services on a global basis.

We have always thought real estate is a people business. No one ever sold a building with e-mail. Be "on the street" so you can talk personally to your sellers and buyers. Create a meaningful relationship.

Binswanger is now in its third generation. Our breadth of services reaches all continents. We are extremely proud of our alliance partners.

To paraphrase Robert Browning, we have always believed that "a man's reach should exceed his grasp, or what is heaven for?" That is, mediocrity is not acceptable. Always do the very best you can.

FOCUS ON LOCATION AND EXECUTION

STEVE BOLLENBACH

Steve Bollenbach is president
and CEO of Hilton Hotels Corporation.

Everybody who has anything to do with the real estate business knows that location is a critical issue, particularly in our hotel business. Where there's a limited supply, we're going to do very well.

Donald Trump also has executed on that notion. With his expertise and well-known name, he could develop anywhere in the world. But if you think about how he's done his best developments over the years, he's focused on the United States, with a sharper focus on New York, and then within New York's Midtown. And he concentrated on the best pieces of real estate in Midtown—the Plaza Hotel, the General Motors Building, his own office complex on Fifth Avenue, and property along Central Park. All those things were good executions of what is obvious to any developer, but everybody doesn't always do it. His success comes from that energy and that focus on execution.

DEVELOP IN AN AREA
WHERE GROWTH IS COMING

ROBERT BOYKIN

Robert Boykin is CEO of Boykin Lodging Company,
a New York Stock Exchange real estate investment trust
specializing in hotels. Based in Cleveland, Ohio, the company
has been involved in the development, management,
and ownership of hotels since 1959.

The best advice I ever got about real estate came from my father, William J. Boykin, who founded Boykin Lodging Company. He said, "Always develop in an area where growth is coming. If you are a little early, or a little wrong in some way, the growth will bail you out. If you develop where growth has been and growth is not continuing, when you are wrong, you are wrong forever." He was right.

MAINTAIN YOUR INTEGRITY;
BE PATIENT; DO YOUR DUE DILIGENCE;
DEPEND ON LOCAL PEOPLE

DAVID BRAUSE

David Brause is president of Brause Realty, Inc.

I am part of a family-owned business. My grandfather started Brause Realty in 1927; my grandmother, now in her nineties, still comes to the office daily; my father is part of any significant deal; and I have siblings, aunts, and cousins involved in the business too. We've had the majority of the assets we own for thirty, forty, and even fifty years. Our business philosophy is the direct opposite of flipping highly leveraged assets.

Although much of what I know I have learned from my family, I feel strongly that anyone involved in a family enterprise should work somewhere else first to gain his or her own experience and insight. My father still remembers the buildings and tenants he canvassed at the brokerage firm where he worked before he joined our company.

I started working for Goldman Sachs in 1992, and during the two years I was there, the environment was intense, but it was a great opportunity to learn the real estate business from some of the top creative minds in the industry. The "street smarts" element, which has traditionally been so essential to success in real estate, must be enhanced by experience and education in business and legal fields.

There are four tenets I have learned from my family:

1. *The single biggest asset of any company or individual in this business is integrity*. Reputation is key. You can do nothing worse than sully your name. I believe that Brause gets business because we have a name that means something. When a broker finds three buildings he likes and one is ours, I think he chooses Brause because he knows how we do business. We're small and can make decisions very quickly, we're honest, and we treat people with respect.

2. *You must be patient*. It's so easy to be overeager and charge into a deal because you want to wrap it up. Take time before making large decisions. The perspective that comes from "breathing" before one gets back to a prospective tenant can make all the difference.

3. *There is no substitute for due diligence*. To this day, my father reads every lease our firm enters into. Before any building acquisition, every single lease must be reviewed. Yes, there are lawyers involved and that is technically their

job, but he believes—and I do, too—that there is nothing like knowing the full story of a property, right down to the basic maintenance contracts.

4. *When you move out of your home territory, it is important to hire local people as your attorneys, architects, brokers, and so on.* It is a truism, of course, that real estate is all about location, and from that truism you can extrapolate that it is a local business. Especially if you come from a large metropolitan market like New York City and are moving into a smaller one, you do well not to appear as a hotshot know-it-all. You achieve that by listening, and I mean *really* listening. Rather than march in and announce, "Here's what we're going to do to put your community on the map," hear what the community leaders and even the local citizens identify as their greatest need.

Our company was involved in a development project in Saratoga Springs, New York, that is a wonderful case in point. Because we were able to create a cooperative atmosphere with the local community, our trade-offs came to be seen as benefits, not merely necessities. As a result, the project won a prestigious award from the local historical preservation agency.

Although there are very few barriers of entry into the real estate business, *staying* in the business requires hard work. In a lot of ways, it's almost like a marriage. While the deals are boiled down to legal contracts, long-term success requires assiduous attention not only to the clauses of those contracts, but also to the needs of all parties involved. Winning takes work, 24-7, but the rewards are worth every hour, day, month, and year of effort.

REAL ESTATE AUCTIONS OFFER BENEFITS TO INVESTORS, WHETHER THEY ARE BUYING OR SELLING

JOHN BROWN

John Brown is chief operating officer of Express Auction, one of the top real estate auction firms in the country.

The best real estate advice I ever received was to consider auctions as a way to buy and sell commercial and investment properties.

Auctions have long been associated with the sale of foreclosures and distressed properties. That is true, but auctions are also a viable and increasingly popular method for buying and selling premium properties as well. The National Auctioneers Association reported that live auctions of commercial real estate increased 4.9 percent in 2005, following an 11.1 percent jump in 2004. Very quietly, the auction market for real estate has grown to $65 billion–plus in yearly sales, and a National Association of Realtors study predicts a staggering one in every three

23

properties will be sold using the auction method by 2010. Multiunit residential buildings, town homes, industrial facilities, development sites, vacant land, office buildings, retail centers, hotels, restaurants, and nightclubs have all been sold at auction recently.

AUCTIONS CREATE A SENSE OF URGENCY

Once a seller decides to market a property via auction, the owner and auction firm decide on a date for the auction. The firm then markets the property with an urgency in order to create a groundswell of interest from potential buyers to attend and bid on auction day. The auction creates a sense of urgency among buyers, who understand that this property will be sold on a specific date. This helps bring serious bidders to the auction who realize that the seller is motivated and serious about moving the property. Buyers head into the auction understanding the terms of the deal, minimum bids, and having had an opportunity to inspect the property and perform their due diligence.

In the end, it's a win-win for buyers and sellers. Ideally, sellers want to make double the market value of a property, while buyers want to pay one-tenth of the market value. Wouldn't we all! The truth is that auctions typically show the current market value for a property and produce a buyer willing to pay it. Moreover, the process happens in sixty days, not six months or two years.

Auction Firms are Real Estate Professionals

As live real estate auctions have grown in popularity, the firms conducting the auctions have evolved to offer a range of services that rival traditional real estate brokerage firms. These are licensed professionals specializing in commercial real estate who have the ability to go beyond the mere implementation of the auction and its mechanics.

Once an auction firm is given a listing, the auction house can handle the entire transaction, from the due diligence and research to closing. Along the way, commercial real estate auction firms work with owners to assess the market, structure the form and terms of sale, deal with any legal or other technical issues, and prepare the marketing plan, advertising copy, and information packet, which can include comparables, demographics, and the economy of the area. The auction firm solicits and vets interest and on the day of the auction, runs the auction as well as ensures a smooth closing process. After a bid is accepted and the contract is signed, auction firms such as Express Auction stay involved in shepherding the sale through to settlement.

Traditional Brokers Work with Real Estate Auction Firms

As auctions have become more mainstream in the commercial real estate industry, there has been an increase in the number of traditional real estate brokerage firms that are now partnering with real estate–licensed auction firms. The traditional broker can now offer a property owner an auction service as one option for the sale of the property.

AUCTIONS WORK IN UP AND DOWN MARKETS

Real estate investors often wonder if auctions work better in an up or a down market, and if auctions favor the buyer or the seller in one market or another. When real estate is hot and it's a seller's market, the seller has the leverage no matter what method is used for the sale. The converse is true in a buyer's market.

There are benefits to auctions in each type of market, though.

In a strong seller's market, auctions help maximize price and ensure that owners receive top dollar for their property since the entire buying audience knows about the opportunity through the intensive marketing campaigns. In a slow market, however, sellers still benefit from the speed of the sale—and the value that comes with having money in hand to reinvest much sooner and eliminating continuing mortgage, taxes, and maintenance payments.

In a buyer's market when there is a glut of property, the auction tends to freeze the market and focus its attention on the auction property. Basically the buyers say, "Hey, I'm going to wait until the auction before I make any offers on similar properties in the area because the auctioned property might be my best deal." No matter what the economy or market, auctions provide a number of real benefits for sellers and buyers:

Speed of Sale. An auction can take a property from list to close in less than ninety days, which reduces carrying costs of a property during its disposition and in a downward market allows a seller to sell before the value depreciates.

Seller Sets the Terms. By presenting terms such as no contingencies; "as is, where is" sale; no warranties; substantial "hard money" deposit; and thirty-day close to the bidding public, the only variable the bidders will be able to set is the amount bid.

Valuation. Both academic studies and our own experience have shown that properties sell for higher prices at auction than they do in a negotiated transaction. This is due at least in part to the forced market reaction that comes with a predetermined sale date.

Transparency. Sellers and buyers know the whole auction process is transparent—the timing of an auction is guaranteed, the rules of the auction are fixed, and the bids are made publicly.

Wider Audience. An auctioneer's proprietary method of advertising and marketing enables a very large universe of buyers to be reached . . . and thus reveals the true market value of the property.

Win-Win for Buyer/Seller. The buyer of a property at auction is also a winner because he avoids protracted negotiations, is afforded a level playing field, and has the confidence of knowing that the price paid is the minimum necessary to buy the property.

Real estate auctions offer benefits to real estate investors, whether they are buying or selling.

INVEST IN SINGLE-FAMILY RENTAL HOUSES

ROBERT J. BRUSS

Robert J. Bruss has written the weekly syndicated Real Estate Mailbag question-and-answer real estate column for more than twenty years. He is the author of *The Smart Investor's Guide to Real Estate* and coauthor with Dr. William Pivar of the college textbook *California Real Estate Law*.

The best real estate advice I ever received came from two sources. The first was *How I Turned $1,000 into a Million in Real Estate—in My Spare Time* by William Nickerson, a paperback book I bought in a Sydney, Australia, hotel gift shop in 1963.

That book ruined the rest of my vacation. I couldn't put it down, even as I visited the beautiful Fiji Islands, Tahiti, and Hawaii on my return trip. It was the most fascinating book I had ever read, and it later became a best seller and changed thousands of readers' lives, including mine, because it gave a blueprint for real estate investment success.

Bill Nickerson revealed in detail how he and his wife,

Lucille, started investing in one small fix-up rental property and pyramided their tax-deferred wealth into millions of equity dollars. Today, only a few public libraries still have that great book. Used copies now cost as much as $100.

That book provided the formula for my real estate investment success. I started by acquiring a three-family triplex, borrowing the $5,000 down payment from my parents (yes, I paid the $5,000 back!), and pyramiding that investment into apartment buildings.

I briefly detoured for a few years by selling investment properties as a real estate broker in San Francisco. But I quickly discovered that while real estate sales commissions provide immediate income, long-term security is provided by real estate investments.

The second source of the best real estate advice I ever received came about in an unusual way. In 1972, I was at the coffee shop counter at the Sheraton Princess Kaiulani Hotel in Honolulu, reading a real estate newspaper article. A Pan Am pilot sitting next to me said, "I see you're interested in real estate. So am I."

That began our conversation about which type of real estate was the best investment. He favored single-family rental houses and told me about an amazing real estate seminar he had recently attended.

I cannot overemphasize the importance of taking every real estate course possible, especially when starting out in real estate investing. I've taken virtually all the real estate courses offered by our local California community college (College of San Mateo), later taught many of those courses, and even coauthored (with Professor William Pivar) a college textbook on California real estate law, now in its sixth edition (2006). Whether you enroll in a one-day learning annex class, a weekend seminar, or a semester college course, it is a great way to quickly learn from experienced instructors and avoid making costly real estate investment mistakes.

About a month after I met that Pan Am pilot, I took the seminar he had recommended: "Making It Big on Little Deals" with John Schaub and Jack Miller in Reno, Nevada. I recall the instructors joking that "real estate is no gamble if you know what you're doing." Then they explained why single-family rental houses are the best long-term real estate investments for average investors like that Pan Am pilot and me.

At the time, I owned a modest San Francisco apartment building that I had fixed up (I had personally painted every apartment in my spare time because I couldn't afford to hire a professional painter) and was ready to profitably trade up for a larger property in a tax-deferred 1031 Exchange. Although that Schaub-Miller seminar almost convinced me to switch my strategy from one of tax-deferred pyramiding to larger buildings to a strategy of buying and holding diversified rental houses, I still was not convinced.

However, one evening shortly after dinner, my home phone rang with angry calls from most of the tenants in my apartment building informing me they had no heat! My resident manager had gone out for the evening, and my tenants had my unlisted home phone number (big mistake!). In San Francisco, lack of heat even in August while most of the nation swelters is a big deal. As Mark Twain was credited with saying, "The coldest winter I ever spent was a summer in San Francisco."

The next day, I had the boiler repaired, and my tenants were happy again. But that event convinced me that I didn't want to have all my eggs in one (apartment building) basket, although I watched that basket very carefully. So I decided to follow the Schaub-Miller formula, sell my apartment building, and acquire single-family rental houses instead. That plan paid off big-time!

As Schaub and Miller taught me at their seminar, it is much easier to buy, finance, manage, and profitably resell single-family rental houses than any other type of real estate investment property.

After switching to single-family rental houses, I was able to manage "tenants and toilets" one house at a time. Instead of having employees, I hired independent contractors such as handymen, plumbers, roofers, and others to do work as needed. If a worker performed unsatisfactorily, I didn't call him again. I never had to fire an employee because I had none.

Equally important, when there is a problem at one rental house, it affects only one tenant. Yes, I've had problems such as plugged-up sewer pipes, but the problem didn't affect an entire building of unhappy tenants like that night my apartment building boiler malfunctioned.

Over the years, I've bought and sold many rental houses at substantial profits, frequently carrying back installment sale mortgages for my buyers to create future income for me without any work except depositing the monthly mortgage checks. Often, I sold my rental houses to my tenants on lease options. They got a good deal, with generous rent credits for part of their rent paid to me. My lease-option benefits were higher than normal rents plus, upon sale, mortgage interest income for future years.

I shall always be grateful to William Nickerson for the great advice in *How I Turned $1,000 into a Million in Real Estate—in My Spare Time*. He showed me how to become wealthy by investing in residential real estate.

Equally important, John Schaub (author of *Building Wealth One House at a Time* [McGraw-Hill, 2004]) and Jack Miller taught me that single-family rental houses are the best investment for the average investor because houses are so easy to buy, finance, manage, and profitably sell.

A COMMONSENSE APPROACH TO FORECLOSURE PROPERTIES

M. ANTHONY CARR

M. Anthony Carr has worked in the real estate industry as an investor, agent, real estate trainer, syndicated columnist, and author since 1989. He is the former real estate editor for the *Washington Times* and author of *Real Estate Investing Made Simple: A Commonsense Approach to Building Wealth.*

The best real estate advice I've received is that when you approach a distressed seller to purchase a foreclosure property, you'd be wise to develop a working relationship with that person as soon as possible. Let him know you are there as an investor to help him avoid foreclosure and put cash in his pocket.

Plenty of would-be investors want to profit by purchasing foreclosure properties. They usually get this idea from some late-night television infomercial, and it germinates into an e-mail to me about how to get started. Truly, foreclosures are the way to quick money for those who get the property at the right price or condition and turn around and sell it for a large profit. The challenge is that many times, you're up against several other investors at the court-house steps who want to do the same thing.

Do what others are *not* doing, and you'll increase your profits tremendously. Go for preforeclosures. These are the true diamonds in the rough of residential investment real estate. They are more profitable because you are dealing with distressed owners who are willing to sell the property at a large discount to save themselves from ruined credit, embarrassment, and financial stress. In the foreclosure world, you're working with estate and foreclosure lawyers who have no emotion connected to the transaction whatso-ever. They are looking for one thing—to get as much money for the note as possible, pay off the mortgage, and turn the property over to a new owner.

The first step is to *search for notice of default (NOD) records* at the county courthouse. This document is sent to the owner of a property who has a mortgage in default. The property owner is now headed to foreclosure and has only a few weeks to reinstate the mortgage or lose his home. By investigating these records, you will find the property owner who is willing to negotiate *now* before your competitors move in at the courthouse steps. You can't wait long. The deadline is quickly approaching once the NOD has been issued.

The second step is to *move swiftly to line up an appointment with the owner*. You want to see if he is ready to negotiate a transaction that will allow him to avoid foreclosure, protect his credit, and put money in his pocket.

However, you will be dealing with a plethora of emotions from the property owner—denial (that he is really in big trouble); anger (that you're trying to profit from his financial woes); unrealistic expectations (that you will somehow give him a loan, let him rent back the house, or pay full price for the house). Learn quickly to deal with these emotions—that is, operate from a purely professional, courteous point of view with the offer of helping him through this dilemma.

Your aim is to get the owner's name off the deed and get your name on it, thus stopping the foreclosure by bringing the current note up to date and paying off the old mortgage company (as well as any taxes or liens that may be on the deed).

The third step is to *be properly prepared* before approaching the preforeclosure owner by having lined up the following:

- Acquisition money (cash or a mortgage)
- Refurbishing money (the same as above)
- A reliable home inspector (to find out what fix-up expenses you have to deal with)

- Contractors (ready and able to move on the property in a matter of days)
- A settlement attorney (to do title search and closing)

You want to get cash to the distressed seller, but figuring out the appropriate amount is the challenge. You first need to know how large the loan to value is on the current note (or notes). In your calculations on whether or not the deal will work, you'll need to determine the fair market value of the house (once it's been fixed up), acquisition costs (closing fees, arrearage, etc.), fix-up expenses, marketing fees, and then your profit.

Your target is to make at least 15 to 25 percent on the sale price of the house, or it may not be worth your while. As a preforeclosure investor, you want a large enough profit margin so that once you've acquired the house, a hidden defect doesn't eat up all your gain.

CHOOSE A REAL ESTATE AGENT WISELY

RICH CASTO

Rich Casto is the founder of Real Estate Coaches
and a columnist for *Realty Times*, *Broker Agent* magazine,
FrogPond, and *Broker Agent News*.

The best real estate advice I ever received was to choose
your real estate agent wisely. Remember, marketing and
advertising alone do not sell homes.

When it is time to put your home on the market, whatever your motivation may be, selecting a real estate agent is
your first and most important move, but what should your
selection criteria be? With agents charging up to 7 percent
commission to sell your home, this becomes a critical decision. You want the one agent who is going to command the
highest price for your home and sell it quickly with the
fewest headaches for you.

Here is what you should look for:

1. *Market knowledge*. This agent is teaming with you to
protect your greatest asset, your home. How knowledge-

able is the agent about the market? Ask where he sees interest rates going in the next six to twelve months. What does the supply of homes look like, and what will the future supply be? An educated agent will give his views and quote his sources about the future of the market.

2. *Negotiation skills.* The majority of agents lack this skill. Ask prospective agents to explain step-by-step how they are going to negotiate the highest price for the home—from receipt of the offer to counteroffers until acceptance. Be prepared to see some blank stares. The industry is not well trained here. An agent should understand the importance of working with the buyer's agent because the buyer is critical. This negotiation is not about posturing; it is about win-win. Skilled negotiators back up the counteroffers with evidence proving that the price is an amazing deal for the buyer. Finding an agent with a negotiation plan will be tough but worthwhile.

3. *Pricing strategy.* Too many agents do not understand proper pricing. It does not matter what houses have sold for; what matters is your competition. When you purchased your current home, you did not compare it to houses that were already sold and not on the market. You looked at all the houses in your price range *currently on the market,* and you made your buying decision. Make sure the agent's pricing strategy is based on what buyers are going to compare your home to, including new construction,

because it is competing for your buyer also. An agent who leaves out new construction in the market analysis is over-looking major competition.

4. *Home enhancement*. Without spending extra money, an agent should be able to rearrange your home for ulti-mate viewing. If the agent doesn't do that, he should have a "Property Stager" portfolio to show you before-and-after listing pictures. When competing for that buyer who is going to give you the best price, home enhancement could be the critical piece that sways him or her.

The multiple listing services provide the marketing. Remember when you purchased your home? You most likely looked at all the ones in your price range and chose the one with the most value. When did the property adver-tising come in? Agents who try to win you over with their "marketing plan" truly do not understand what is most important in getting the best price.

FIVE PRINCIPLES TO SUCCESS

18

PHOEBE CHONGCHUA
Phoebe Chongchua is a real estate writer,
realtor with the Guiltinan Group, and veteran television
newscaster based in San Diego, California.

As a national real estate writer, licensed agent, and veteran television newscaster, I have interviewed thousands of people, asking them detailed questions about real estate and how to be successful in it. I've found five key principles.

1. *Get in the real estate game.* In 2006, according to *Forbes* magazine, there were nearly eight hundred billionaires. More than sixty of the billionaires made their wealth in whole or in part in the real estate industry. If you want a chance at being rich, you've got to get in the game.

2. *Buy and hold.* It's contradictory to what we have seen happen in several markets across the U.S. Speculators timing the market bought properties with the intention of flipping for huge profits. While that did sometimes happen, it's

risky business. Wealth isn't usually made overnight in real estate. Buying and holding real estate can create bigger long-term gains.

3. *Never sell; instead do a 1031.* I've spoken with many brokers who assert that when you want to get out of an investment or a commercial property, trading up is the way to go. Using a 1031 Exchange to defer your tax gains not only saves you money but also allows you to buy the next property you want.

4. *Cash reserve trumps cash flow.* Of course, to have both is optimal. But real estate attorney and author William Bronchick told me that cash reserve trumps cash flow. Why? Let's say you have a property that provides $400 cash flow, your monthly mortgage is $1,500, and you have no or very little cash reserve. A one-month vacancy will eat up a little more than a three-month profit. Now, if you have repairs that come due at the same time as that vacancy, you could go broke quickly. But just as in any business, cash reserves can help you survive rough periods. Even if you have $100 negative cash flow but $20,000 in the bank, you're prepared when rocky times hit. The bottom line is to have a cash reserve to sustain the property. In an appreciating market where you have a cash reserve but a small amount of negative cash flow, you'll ultimately do fine.

5. *Be enthusiastic, not overly excited.* When we become overly excited, we often forget to ask the important ques-

tions. Sometimes discretion is replaced by frivolous emotions that make something seem more vital than it is. In real estate, no matter whether you're buying your primary residence or your one-hundredth property, being enthusiastic and diligent about the deal will benefit you. But if you allow yourself to get overly excited, you're likely to miss both the good and the bad points about the property. For instance, when properties have multiple offers and a bidding war ensues, buyers who become overly excited and eager to win the property can find they'll end up paying much more than they bargained for.

LISTEN TO YOUR TELEVISION

FRANK COOK

Frank Cook is a best-selling real estate author whose
books include *21 Things I Wish My Broker Had Told Me*,
You're Not Buying That House Are You?,
and *21 Things Every Home Inspector Should Know*.

The best bit of real estate advice I ever received was from a buyer/broker (Jim Warkinton in northern Virginia), who told me that if I wanted to be successful in real estate, I should watch television.

In his opinion, the best sign that a bull market was beginning to turn was seeing real estate agents on TV who were talking about what a good investment real estate was "right now."

"When real estate agents start selling homes as an 'investment' instead of 'shelter,' you know the market is about to turn," Warkinton said.

According to the agent, prudent, professional real estate investors know how to time the market, and most real estate agents working on the street do not. He considered it a "forest for the trees syndrome"—the closer real estate agents are to the market, and the busier the agents are, the more likely they are to miss the market swing—because they are part of that swing.

By the time they realize that double-digit percentage equity gains are occurring, it's too late to get in at the bottom. In fact, the market may be close to its peak by the time the agent on the street gets a clue. In other words, real estate agents typically jump on the bandwagon just before it breaks and start advertising homes as "great investments."

But, my friend cautioned, that doesn't mean you should avoid getting in.

He points out that most real estate "slumps" are actually no more than a leveling off. Market values don't really deteriorate as much as they stop going up and up. (There are exceptions, of course. If the local big manufacturer suddenly has massive layoffs, values could dive.)

In most markets where there is a slowdown, the worst-case scenario is a slide of between 5 and 10 percent in values, and it usually doesn't last more than eighteen months to two years before the market resumes an upward trend. (Again, there are exceptions. California in the early to mid-1980s hit a slump that took about five years for the market to recover from. There were massive overbuilding and massive speculation, which led to the savings and loan debacle.)

45

By and large, this advice has withstood the test of time, right to today. While there consistently had been dutiful stories in the papers about the expansion in the housing market over the last few years, it wasn't until mid-2005 that real estate agents and the mainstream media really started pumping up the balloon, talking about cabdrivers at cocktail parties bragging about making $50,000 in three months in real estate.

Not five months later you started hearing about housing "cooling off."

WORK WITH WHAT YOU'VE GOT

18

BARBARA CORCORAN

Barbara Corcoran is founder of The Corcoran Group, New York City's leading real estate company, and author of *Use What You've Got and Other Business Lessons I Learned from My Mom* and *If You Don't Have Big Breasts, Put Ribbons on Your Pigtails*.

(Excerpted from the book *If You Don't Have Big Breasts, Put Ribbons on Your Pigtails*, written by Barbara Corcoran and published by Penguin Group. Copyright Barbara Corcoran.)

The story of my million-dollar business starts like this: I borrowed a thousand dollars from a friend. Okay, I didn't borrow it. He gave it to me. And he wasn't a friend. He was a boyfriend. But when I moved into my first apartment on East Eighty-sixth Street with two roommates, I did have a thousand dollars to start a real estate company.

It seemed so simple. There'd be virtually no overhead! I'd probably rent two, maybe even three, apartments a day, and we'd be running at a profit by the second Sunday of every month. "All the rest will be gravy," I told my business partner/boyfriend, Ramóne Simóne. "And we'll share the gravy evenly," he added. Or *almost evenly*—49 percent for me and 51 percent for him. After all, he explained, he was the one risking the money.

I was wiping the counter of the Fort Lee Diner the first time Ramóne walked in. It was a quiet night. There were only a few customers in the diner, and the other waitress, Gloria, had them all. Well, Gloria and her two well-rounded friends. Gloria was built like Dolly Parton with a big bleached-blond swirl of cotton candy hair. Her breasts were the specialty of the house and had the power to lure men off the street, even if they weren't hungry. She could carry six cups of coffee stacked on top of them, and never spill a drop.

Gloria and her dynamic duo had put the Fort Lee Diner on the map, and watching the twins bounce around the diner had become sport in Fort Lee. I was watching her work the front section and, in an effort to feel busy, I was wiping the barren Formica landscape in front of me with a soggy white rag.

The double aluminum doors at the far end of the diner opened and in walked my destiny. I knew he was there before I ever looked up. With his dark skin and jet-black hair, he was unlike the working-class customers who frequented the place. In his blue aviator shades, he was different, probably from a land very far away. At least across the river, I figured. . . .

He ordered a cup of tea, and while I banged in and out of the swinging kitchen door, he sat and sipped it, hardly moving, just watching as I worked my counter. . . . Ramóne told me he was from the "Basque Country." I didn't know if Basque was a town in New Jersey or not, and I suppose my face gave me away. It wasn't just any-place in Spain, he explained, it was the upper echelon of French-Spanish society. . . .

He left sixty-five cents on the counter and offered me a ride home. I didn't need to weigh the options—walk the five blocks to the number 8 Lemoine Avenue bus or be driven home by the man from the Basque Country. "I'm finished at ten," I blurted.

After my shift, I took the diner's concrete steps two at a time. Ramóne was parked at the bottom in a buttercup-yellow Lincoln Continental, the kind with the hump on the back. . . . I opened the door and climbed into a car very different from any I'd ever been in. The seats felt like talcum powder against my arms and smelled expensive, unlike the crunchy seats of Dad's blue station wagon. . . . My family hated Ray on sight, especially my mom, who, contrary to her normally welcoming ways, wanted the Dark Knight out of her house as quickly as possible. "He's much older than you" is all I remember her saying after Ray left. What she didn't say screamed loudly in the silence.

Ray waited outside the diner every night and gave me a ride home. I guess you could say we were dating, though I didn't think of the rides that way. He told me he was a big real estate developer and built houses in every town in New Jersey except mine. I also learned that he was fifteen years older than I and was divorced with three daughters. To me, this all added to the intrigue.

A few months later, Ray said a smart girl like me should be living in the Big City, and to get me started, he offered to pay for a week at the Barbizon Hotel for Women. To my mother's dismay, I jumped at his offer and packed up a few belongings. . . .

Ray gave me some money to go buy myself a "real New York outfit." I bought a purple one . . . I walked out of Bloomingdale's all purple and paraded up Lexington Avenue singing, *"Hey there! Georgy Girl, swinging down the street so fancy free . . ."* I knew I was lookin' good and needed only two more things to stay in New York: a job and an apartment.

The next morning I put on my new outfit and applied for a receptionist's position with the Giffuni Brothers company on Eighty-third and First. Thelma, my interviewer, explained that the Giffuni Brothers were two wealthy landlords who owned a dozen apartment buildings in Manhattan and Brooklyn. She said I'd be in charge of greeting every tenant who called with: "Good morning, Giffuni Brothers."

By the end of the day, I had landed the receptionist's position and by the end of the week I had used the *Village Voice* want ads to find an apartment three blocks away from the office and two girls to share the rent. I moved myself out of the Barbizon Hotel.

My Giffuni Brothers stint introduced me to Manhattan real estate. I wore my purple outfit eight days a week and probably said, "Good morning, Giffuni Brothers" eight hundred times a day. But after a few months of "Good morning, Giffuni Brothers," I eagerly gave Ray my "no overhead" spiel about running at a profit by the second Sunday of every month, and he gave me the $1,000 to start a real estate company. We became partners and named it Corcoran-Simone. My old boss, Joseph Giffuni, said if I could find a tenant for one of his apartments, he'd pay me a whole month's rent as a commission. He showed me the list of apartments they had for rent, and I picked Apartment 3K, the cheapest one-bedroom on the list.

I created my makeshift Corcoran-Simone office on the sofa one of my roommates had borrowed from her parents. My newly installed pink Princess phone sat silent on the double-tiered mahogany end table, as I stared bleary-eyed at the Sunday *New York Times* classified section. According to my count, there were exactly 1,246 one-bedroom apartments advertised. The ads were five or six lines long and the apartments were all priced between $320 and $380 a month. I noticed the best ads among the lot were splashy ones with the bigger, bolder headlines like: "FABULOUS 3!" "RIV VU 1 BR." "TRIPLE MINT!!!" followed by a long list of superlatives.

I worked out the numbers on my steno pad, and realized that the big ads were a lot bigger than my budget. I decided to keep my ad to four lines or less in order to make Ray's $1,000 last a whole month. *But how*, I wondered, *could I make my little ad stand out among the biggies and how was I going to draw someone's eye?*

Stretching my neck and looking up from the paper, I thought about my job at the Fort Lee Diner. *Ah, Gloria! Now she had a gimmick.* On my first day at the diner, I saw Gloria had assets I'd never have, and that night went home to fret to my mother: "And when we weren't busy, Mom, my counter was plain empty. Even when Gloria's station was completely filled, men were *still* asking to sit with Gloria and not me."

"Barbara Ann, you've got a great personality," Mom said, as she balanced Baby Florence on her hip and hung a sheet on the line. "You're going to have to learn to use what you've got. Since you don't have big breasts, why don't you tie some ribbons on your pigtails and just be as sweet as you are?"

And that's how Ray found me two years later, wearing ribbons on my pigtails and offering a cheerful alternative to the big-breasted, tiny-waisted, blond-bombshell Fort Lee sensation. I considered it a personal victory when a customer walked into the diner and asked to sit with "Pigtails." The simple gimmick pulled them to my counter and my sweet talking kept them coming back.

Sitting alone in my apartment with the *New York Times* spread open on my lap, I thought about Mom's advice for competing with Gloria's superlatives, and I knew I needed an attention-grabber for Apartment 3K. *How*, I asked myself, *can I put ribbons on a typical one-bedroom in four lines or less and make it stand out from the other 1,246 apartments?*

I took a deep breath and picked up my pink Princess phone. "Hello, Mr. Giffuni," I began. "I've been thinking about your one-bedroom on the third floor, and I think I have a way to rent it for twenty dollars more each month." I had his attention. I told him how Apartment 3K's living room was like every other living room in every other apartment in every other building in New York and convinced him that if he put up a wall separating the living room from the dining alcove, he'd really have something different! Mr. Giffuni hesitated, giving it some thought, and then said he'd have the wall installed that week. I phoned my ad into the paper.

The following Sunday, my first four-line ad (**bold** print counted for two lines) appeared in the *New York Times*:

1 BR + DEN $340
Barbara Corcoran
212.355.3550

It wasn't a big ad like the others, but it sure offered something more. Why would *anyone* settle for a one-bedroom, when for the same price you could get a one-bedroom with a den?

That Sunday, the calls began. And on Monday I rented my first apartment.

Mom's Lesson #1: If you don't have big breasts, put ribbons on your pigtails.

The Lesson Learned About Using What You've Got

I didn't have a big chest, but I did have a nice personality, a great smile, and the gift of gab. All I needed was my mother's cue to begin using them to my advantage. That was my first lesson in sales.

Although the apartment I advertised wasn't any bigger than the hundreds of others advertised that Sunday, my ad caught attention because it offered something extra—one

54

more room. My "1 BR + DEN" ad enabled the customer to focus on the *perceived* benefit of more space, and the overwhelming response to the ad gave me a lot more bang for my advertising buck.

Good salesmanship is nothing more than maximizing the positive and minimizing the negative. Although your competition might offer something you can't match, that doesn't matter. What matters is that you identify and play up what you've got.

THE FIRST OFFER IS USUALLY THE BEST

RICHARD COURTNEY

Richard Courtney, author of *Buyers Are Liars and Sellers Are Too*, is the principal broker for Fridrich and Clark Realty's Music Row office in Nashville, Tennessee. He serves on the board of directors of the National Association of Realtors and has received the President's Award for his work in legislative affairs.

It was Karl Haury, one of the innovators in condominium construction in Nashville in the 1960s, who told me to work the first offer as if it would be the last because, oddly enough, it usually would be the best offer.

At first I didn't believe it. I was young, green, and cocky enough to share the confidence of some of my clients who were selling their properties that there would always be a better offer later on. Many sellers feel that if the first offer is received easily, that means there is an ocean of buyers who will pay a higher price for their property. But sometimes the asking price is based as much on the seller's needs as on the value of the property. And in those cases, the sell-

THE BEST REAL ESTATE ADVICE I EVER RECEIVED

ers who turned down an early offer have come back to me to ask, "Whatever happened to those people who made that offer three months ago?" And in almost every instance, I have had to say, "They bought something else even though they didn't like it as much as your property. It's a shame we couldn't have worked it out."

A seller and his agent should coddle, nurture, massage, and appreciate the first offer. Make a counteroffer, but make it a fair one. An offer received on the first days a property is on the market is more valuable than any other offer that will be made. The next offer may not come until after a price reduction. Receiving the first offer means you have achieved your first goal—finding an interested buyer. Now sell the property.

CHOOSE A GOOD PARTNER

LESTER CROWN

Lester Crown is chairman of Henry Crown and Company,
an investment firm whose holdings include stakes in Maytag,
the New York Yankees, and real estate.

The best real estate advice I ever received pertains not just
to real estate but to any transaction—you can't make a
good deal with a bad partner.

ADD VALUE TO YOUR REAL ESTATE INVENTORY

GIL DEZER

Gil Dezer is part of the father-son team of Dezer Development and president of Trump Grande Ocean Resort and Residences. He is one of the nation's youngest developers of luxury high-rise real estate.

There's no question that the older you are, the more experience you have. My father has been through it all and seen it all and knows how to handle every situation. Being around him allows me to pick up on his instincts, and this has provided me with the experience to impart certain real estate advice that I feel is essential to survive in the industry:

Hold on to property. Hold, hold, hold—don't sell if you don't need the money.

Reinvest and upgrade. Always upgrade your real estate inventory by buying something better after you sell, while reinvesting your earnings with 1031 Exchanges.

Market properly. When we were seeking to sell for the highest amount per square foot, we realized that branding was the fastest way to bring credibility and value to a project. So, to meet our goals for high-priced sales of multiple units, we created the ultimate value by getting together with Donald Trump. His name, expertise, and marketing draw gave us instant value and credibility in a market that was new to me. Of course, displaying the product in the most beautiful sales pavilion ever created was a must in order to back up the expectations one would have when entering a Trump property. It also gave our buyers a taste of the quality work we do and a little hint of how their new home would feel. This branding concept of marketing has been done for many types of products, but has been seldom used in real estate.

Make it look good. People will pay more for a higher perceived value. When *selling* a property, keep the property in tip-top shape so that a future buyer will feel that he has less of a maintenance problem when he closes. When *purchasing* a property, look for quick cosmetic fixes that mask potential future issues unless, of course, it's a really good deal!

Ultimately, the money is in being able to deal with the headaches!

CHOOSE A TRUSTWORTHY PARTNER

THOMAS E. DOBROWSKI

Thomas E. Dobrowski is the former managing director
of real estate and alternative investments at
General Motors Asset Management.

I have found that, by far, the best real estate advice I ever
received—which was quickly affirmed by my experience—is to carefully pick partners with integrity who are
relationship oriented.

Real estate is a cyclical business with many factors con-
tributing to success. Location and asset quality are frequently cited as the most important considerations of a real
estate investment, but I would argue that the most important consideration is the choice of partners.

Throughout the course of my thirty-year career in the
investment management business, I have had the privilege
of partnering with many of the icons in the real estate
industry, including builders, developers, financial engineers, and smart entrepreneurs. In addition to the required

experience with one or more specific property types (office, industrial, retail, multifamily, lodging, etc.), two noteworthy characteristics that many of them had in common were a high level of integrity and the recognition of the value of a long-term relationship. This almost always resulted in a fair deal structure and provided access to an ongoing flow of new ideas and attractive opportunities.

The real estate industry in the United States, as well as in many other countries, is controlled by a relatively small number of players. There are far more providers of capital than there are providers of real estate expertise with a high level of integrity and the recognition of the value of a long-term relationship. The right choice of partners not only improves the likelihood of strong financial rewards but also makes life easier when things don't go as planned. The bottom line: good partners make real estate fun.

SUCCESS IN REAL ESTATE
COMES THROUGH HARD WORK
AND DIRECT SALES CONTACTS

CROSBY DOE

Crosby Doe is a partner at Mossler & Doe, a firm he founded
with David Mossler. The firm represents and sells estates
and historic and architectural residential properties,
primarily in Southern California.

The best real estate advice I ever received came from the
first broker I ever worked for, a man named Larry
O'Rourke. At that time, 1973, I was twenty-six years old.
He told me that for salespeople, success in real estate is
based on the numbers. How many people have you called?
How many houses have you shown? How many listings
have you called on? Success in real estate doesn't just fall
out of the sky. It is about hard work and direct contacts.

Let me give you an example. I identified one thousand
houses that were of historic and architectural importance.
I made contact with the owners of those homes. If one

person moves every ten years or so, that means every year there are one hundred "houses of interest" coming up for sale, and I have them all. It's been that simple ever since.

By 1976, I joined Bob Crane & Associates. Crane gave me the opportunity to found an architectural division within his company. It was the very first division in the real estate business specializing exclusively in historic proper-ties. Crane's concern, even though we were doing well after nine months, was that we could not make a living selling just "architecture." He wasn't sure there was enough great architecture to make a career out of it. It spurred me on to prove him wrong, and now I have five thousand houses of importance and there are dozens of architectural specialists in Los Angeles.

Even though I own the company, my passion is still real estate sales on the front line.

APPROACH THE BUSINESS WITH CANDOR AND FORTHRIGHT DEALING

MARC ELLMAN

Marc Ellman is president of Ellman Realty Advisors, whose focus is tenant representation and commercial leasing in Manhattan.

Real estate is a complex, high-energy business. What contributes to success varies according to the role you play—investor or broker.

For investors, in addition to the standard adage of location, location, location, returns depend on having good timing, deep pockets, and sound financing relationships. The market inevitably is cyclical. The investor who makes money is the one who has the ability to ride out the waves. Sure, it would be nice to be able to spot the lows and buy then, just as in the equities market. But when an investor buys at what turns out to be a top price, with the financial capability to hold on, he or she can watch the market fall, bottom out, start back up, and break the former high so it will still reveal itself as a good investment. The point is, it can be a waiting game.

As far as brokers are concerned, it is my strong opinion that the real estate brokerage industry gets a bad rap. Good brokers are not all about making money. And even if they are, the best way for one to make money is to create an atmosphere of trust and reliability. In the two-plus decades I've been in the commercial office leasing business, I've represented both landlords and tenants, although I've spent more time with the latter. There have even been instances when I represented both sides simultaneously. How can that be possible? From a strictly legal standpoint, the answer is, of course, full disclosure, but it is far more than that. Full candor and forthright dealing, even if your client and/or customer doesn't want to hear what you have to say, are tantamount. Nervous prospective tenants want to know how I can represent them if the landlord is paying the fee. The answer is that both parties know how I work and for whom I'm working, every time.

Having a basic sales aptitude, of course, is an important underpinning of succeeding in the real estate brokerage business. Ultimately, after the research is done, the amenities, location, and prices are compared, office space sells itself. The good real estate broker does exactly the same—sells himself or herself. How? By getting "inside" the business and sometimes even the personal preferences of the clients. Know how they work. Know what the hot buttons are. Refuse to impart information or advice if you aren't the most competent person to do so. Recently a customer called again and again, asking me to tell him what to do about some needed retrofitting. When I refused, he got angry and accused me of passing the buck. I stuck to my guns and insisted that he call his architect and his engineer, the people who knew the most about retrofitting. In time, he saw why.

In any deals I handle, my strongest advice is to never "fumble on the two-yard line." From the very beginning do thorough research, present complete information, and build absolute trust. Then, when a transaction is being completed, no new problems arise that might derail it because the party I am representing is fully cognizant of the compromises that may have been necessary to consummate the deal.

When I started my firm, the first thing I did was to put my name on the door. There was no way I was going to hide behind a layer of various corporate entities that are hard to pin down or vague, spin-doctor descriptions of what I am capable of doing. My customers and clients know that, and I believe that's why they are my book of business. And that's why so much of my business now comes from referrals and repeat business.

DON'T FOLLOW THE CROWD

BLANCHE EVANS

Blanche Evans is editor of *Realty Times*, the Internet's largest independent real estate news service, and author of *Bubbles, Booms, and Busts*. She has been named one of the "25 Most Influential People in Real Estate" by *Realtor* magazine.

Like any other investment, real estate comes down to risk versus reward. If you want to make money with housing, you have to sift through the current data to spot opportunities, go against conventional wisdom, and do what others are unwilling to do. Get there first.

How do you do that? Skate to where you think the puck is going to be. Hockey legend Wayne Gretzky didn't know it, but when he revealed his strategy for success, he was giving great advice for real estate.

Let's say you want to build wealth through owning housing, but you don't quite know how to go about it. Start with learning the market conditions.

Seventy percent of Americans are homeowners, but in

2005 nearly 36 percent of the homes sold were to investors and owners of second homes. Most of those purchases were made with high-risk, low-entry adjustable rate mortgages; in other words, quite a number of people bought bigger, more expensive homes than they would have if they had fixed-rate loans. That means one-third of the homes sold in 2005 will be non-owner occupied, with a strong absorption in the higher-end markets, leaving perfectly good older homes behind and depressed.

Now consider this. While buyers piled into luxury with their low-cost loans, there were record apartment conversions to condos, which depleted the inventory of valuable workforce rentals. Condos overall appreciated faster than single-family homes in 2005. Unimproved older homes devalued in some areas, while in others, affordable workforce housing was torn down, remodeled, or otherwise regentrified into luxury townhomes, high-rises, McMansions, or other high-priced housing.

Meanwhile, interest rates are rising, loans are tightening, the government is cooling housing through federal and legislative means, and the luxury party is coming to a temporary end.

There is too much money chasing luxury homes, while a serious need for workforce housing is being unmet. And that spells opportunity. Is it smarter to buy more luxury housing at this point (with an adjustable rate) or to take advantage of still-low fixed rates and buy affordable housing—multi- and single-family?

You could probably argue the case either way, but ask yourself—where is the puck, or opportunity, going to be?

If you're going to make money at real estate, you have to get there first. But you have to get to where the next boom is going to be, not where it already is. You're taking the risk that you're right, and if you are, the rewards will be higher than if you followed the crowd.

The alternative is to pay someone else a premium to take your risks for you, but that's even riskier. You don't want to buy at the top of the market because it could be years before the market reaches a new top and you can profit. Although it seems counterintuitive, you have to be willing to do what others won't do, and that is to position yourself out there alone where you think the next big opportunity is going to be.

So, learn everything there is to know about property management, and invest in older workforce housing near vital city centers and public transportation. Hold off on the gentrification, but make the properties clean, safe, pleasant, and livable to attract good tenants. Sit on the properties until they generate enough profits to buy more. Those semi-luxury properties will become available one day, and many at a discount, so be ready to buy when others are desperate to bail out because they bought more than they could afford.

You can really feel good about this kind of real estate investing. Making affordable housing available is a great community service, and it doesn't hurt that you can make money at it too.

EMPHASIZE QUALITY AND BRANDING

26

MICHAEL FASCITELLI

Michael Fascitelli is president of Vornado Realty Trust,
a fully integrated real estate investment trust
and one of the largest owners and managers
of real estate in the United States.

Always go with quality. Buy quality products, build a high-quality brand name, and hire top-quality staff. When we were looking at the GM Building on Fifth Avenue across from the southeast corner of Central Park in New York, Donald Trump said, "I think you should go for it." Then we passed on it, and he ended up buying it because he said it was a unique, high-quality building. If you buy quality, which is very scarce, you'll come out better.

The next important step is to build a brand and a product that can command a premium. The Trump brand and name, for example, can command a premium of a couple of hundred dollars per square foot in the condo world. He built that brand name by focusing on and doing well in

New York and then broadening the brand to Chicago, Florida, and other markets.

Always hire the best staff you can. Hire someone who has a pleasant, attractive personality because it's part of your image and ultimately part of your brand name.

MAKE THE MOST OF THE INTERNET

DEBBIE FERRARI

Debbie Ferrari is a top real estate broker in Orange County,
California, and the 2006 vice president of the National Council
of Exchangors. Her pioneering 1,000-page Web site is the
most-awarded Realtor site in the United States.

The best real estate advice I ever received came in 1996 when we saw our very first Web page, and my husband, Bill, said, "This new Internet thing is going to be the future of real estate; you've got to become part of it." Then he added, "On second thought, you should always *dominate* all other Realtors on the Internet in your marketing area."

I took his advice, and today, when 80 percent of consumers use the Internet to hunt for homes and Realtors, my site comes up number one, ahead of all other Realtors in Orange County, California (3 million population). There are three reasons why our site comes up first: (1) My site, www.debbieferrari.com, was one of the earliest Realtor Web sites. We started the site in 1996 when we realized early on that the Internet would become a huge marketing tool for Realtors. (2) With nearly one thousand pages of content, my site is one of the most comprehensive Realtor Web sites and contains information consumers want and need when considering a real estate purchase, sale, rental, or exchange. (3) Search engines such as Google like sites that refresh themselves. We add new content almost every day, often entire pages at a time.

When people search for "Orange County Real Estate," "Orange County Realtor," "Orange County Property Exchange," and many other top search terms on Google, AOL, and other search engines, www.debbieferrari.com comes up first.

Following Bill's advice to dominate the market in my region has been worth many millions of dollars to me. It has also made me nationally famous for my site, the most-awarded Realtor site in the United States.

AIM HIGH AND TRUST YOUR INSTINCTS

ROBERT L. FREEDMAN

Robert L. Freedman is president and CEO of GVA Williams Real
Estate Company, a full-service commercial real estate brokerage, consulting, and strategic organization headquartered in
New York City. He developed GVA Worldwide, a global partnership
organization serving 120 business capitals on five continents.

As a young commercial real estate broker in the early
1970s, I generated business through a technique known
as canvassing—cold calls to prospects and unsolicited drop-
ins. I worked with small- to medium-sized tenancies in midtown Manhattan, and I achieved a level of professionalism
in taking these tenants through the intricacies of deal making. I identified potentially suitable space and negotiated
terms and conditions mutually acceptable to landlord and
tenant, with one notable exception—security. Most of my
prospects were economically marginal tenancy, and secur-
ing the lease emerged as the critical success factor in the
transaction. Landlords were loath to enter into leases with

such tenants, and the tenants, who did not have the economic standing to post significant security, could not induce their banks to issue letters of credit on a cost-effective basis. Many transactions never concluded because of that dilemma.

Aim high. At my year-end review, my sales manager said he was pleased with my work ethic, creativity, work product, and entrepreneurial spirit, but they had yet to be fully reflected in my performance. Scrutinizing my appearance and bearing, he blurted out, "Your mother didn't buy you $50 ties [in 1974 dollars] to work with little [expletive deleted] tenants that no one ever heard of."

That remark really resonated. He was telling me to set my sights higher, to pursue Fortune 500 tenancy and larger transactions because he believed I could compete at that level. That changed my business dynamic and leveraged me up.

Trust your instincts. Another great lesson I learned is to trust my instincts. A classic example of this principle involves a major financial institution and a building it took back pursuant to a deed in lieu of foreclosure.

The institution had written down the asset to $6 million and assigned it for disposition to a wholly owned subsidiary and real estate development arm of the institution. This twenty-four-story office building, circa 1911, aggregating 230,000 square feet, was situated at the virtual epicenter of the proposed Forty-second Street Redevelopment Project, whose designated developer was a quasi-government agency known as the New 42. The building, however, was out of the purview of the public sector. It should be noted that Forty-second Street between Seventh and Eighth Avenues was a veritable poster child for urban blight and decay.

The client for whom we managed the asset received an unsolicited proposal of $18 million. The client asked for our counsel, expressing a preference to sell the asset and migrate it off the company's books.

We investigated the asset and pending developments with respect to the New 42. At that time, the office leasing market was trending up, and critical mass was starting to evolve on Forty-second Street. Our two neighbors, the New Amsterdam Theatre and the Forest City Ratner Project, were in discussions with Disney and Madame Tussaud's, respectively. The building, though not a municipally designated landmark, was on the National Register of Historic Places and was eligible for historic tax credits.

I asked client senior management if we could participate in the project as a principal, not as a broker. They declined, citing conflict of interest, but paid rapt attention as we set out development scenarios that would yield astronomical returns on investment.

We embarked on the project, anticipating a "retailtainment" base with a boutique office building atop. The tenancy would be entertainment based, a compatible fit with this organic and reinvented "urban entertainment zone." We and our client fully appreciated that the project was about "equity in the brand" for a prospective tenant as much as the cost structure of a real estate transaction.

After identifying target prospects, we contacted CEOs and board-level executives rather than the corporate real estate function. We concentrated our advertising budget (well over $100,000) in one media vehicle—*Variety*, known as the bible of the entertainment industry—with a two-page spread "pop-up" of a whimsical and cartoonish Red Grooms–like depiction of Forty-second Street.

An asset that had been written down to $6 million sold for approximately $165 million, accompanying a capital expenditure of only $28 million (reflecting the federal tax credit).

My takeaway from this is quite simple: trust your instincts, even if they do not meet with client approval at the inception.

EMBRACE CHANGE

DOUG FRYE

Doug Frye is president and CEO of Colliers Macaulay Nicolls.

Our industry has always evolved slowly, giving a significant advantage to the early adopters who embrace change. Look beyond the following truisms to accelerate your success!

1. *Real estate is a relationship business*. Not true. Real estate is an identity business. People don't do business with people they like; they do business with people who have an identity that can help them achieve their personal goals and objectives. Being well liked is a bonus, but at best it is only a tiebreaker.

2. *Think location, location, location*. It is always nice to have the best location, but in today's world, the key is specialization, specialization, specialization. Whether you're buying, selling, or providing services, there is a good chance that your competition is 100 percent focused on a specific product type, market, or business line. If you are a

generalist, you will come in second, finishing behind the specialist every time.

3. *Access to information has leveled the playing field.* Actually the glut of information has just shifted the emphasis to speed and quality of execution. People with the experience to quickly identify and extract the important data will be the front–runners in the game.

TREAT PEOPLE WITH RESPECT

D. KENT GALE

D. Kent Gale is chairman of The Daniel Gale Agency,
Long Island's largest independent nonfranchised residential
real estate broker. The Daniel Gale Agency was established
in 1922 by Daniel Gale, father of Kent Gale and
grandfather of The Gale Company's Stan Gale.

When I started working for my father's company, The
Daniel Gale Agency, in 1937, business was conducted
with a handshake. Things have changed a lot since then. But
integrity and a focus on people—those things still matter.

My father, Daniel Gale, was full of ideas. My son Stan,
founder of The Gale Company, inherited that trait, I might
add. Even though we had a family cigar business, my
father had the idea to sell insurance policies to commuters
on the train to Manhattan. He was so good at it that he
decided to expand into real estate and set up his own company in 1922. He set his sights on a property he loved, a
beautiful hilly piece of land in Huntington, Long Island,

near where we lived. It was still mostly rural then. But he could see that people would want to live there, and he found a partner. They ended up making a great deal of money—those lots sold like hotcakes. He had vision and the confidence to follow it.

My father also had a lot of respect for people and treated them well. I learned a key lesson one day while working with my father in the office. A man came in wearing knickers, I recall, and he cut a rather unimpressive figure. But my father spent two hours talking with him. I could hear bits of the conversation, which didn't even touch on real estate. When the man left, I asked my father why he had spent so much time with this fellow.

My father laughed and reminded me not to judge someone by appearance but to give all a fair hearing. People will surprise you, he said. I later learned this fellow was actually one of the most influential men on Long Island. Indeed, he owned a castle!

When I entered the military in 1941, that advice stayed with me and helped guide me through my five years of service. Indeed, two successful companies arose from that dictum—The Daniel Gale Agency, which I took over in 1964, and my son Stan's firm, The Gale Company.

It all starts with people—those who work for you and those who work with you, your customers. Treat them well. Treat them with respect.

MAKE INTEGRITY YOUR REPUTATION

STANLEY C. GALE

Stanley C. Gale is chairman and CEO of The Gale Company,
one of the largest privately held commercial real estate firms
in the world with a portfolio exceeding 60 million square feet.
The Gale Company has invested more than $3 billion on behalf
of its investment partners since the company's inception
in 1985. He is the son of D. Kent Gale.

I learned from my father and grandfather that in real estate
your word is your bond. No contract is worth more than
a handshake. My grandfather started our residential real
estate company, The Daniel Gale Agency, in 1922, and
under my father's tutelage it became a billion-dollar brokerage company. It remains independent and highly trusted
among the most discerning buyers and sellers on Long
Island's Gold Coast. The longevity and success are testa-
ments to the importance of honor in this business.

Integrity *is* a differentiator.

Love the property. I am not a believer in many of the so-called truisms that abound in real estate, especially commercial real estate. One such truism is that "you should never fall in love" with a property—at least not until you run the numbers—or that real estate is reducible to "bricks and sticks." This is nonsense.

I *have* to fall in love with a property. And I'm not ashamed to say that I believe in love at first sight. If I don't experience that unmistakable shock, that instant recognition, if I don't fall in love with a property, then there is no deal. I can't emphasize enough that the Gale way is to love a property and be proud of it and want to make a difference with it. A property is so much more than bricks and sticks.

Visualize the outcome. I also have to be able to visualize the outcome from the first second I see a property—who my partner will be, what the time frame will be, who will lease it. And if I can't sketch out the whole transaction on something simple like a cocktail napkin, it will never work on an Argus run. That has led some people to question why I pay what they consider a premium for high-quality properties. But they're stuck in the "now," while I've already visualized what the property will be—what the property's true value will be in the end. As Wayne Gretzky's father advised him, "Go to where the puck is going, not where it's been."

Meet face-to-face. I also learned from my family that nothing can replace a face-to-face meeting. I traveled to South Korea forty-five times while cementing the partnership that made The Gale Company the primary developer of New Songdo City, the $25 billion project that is the largest private real estate development in the world. That's more than 1,300 hours spent on airplanes—and lots of kimchi—but the close personal relationships made it all worthwhile.

Share the risks. Another "truism" I have found to be untrue insists, "Don't do business with friends." I say, do business *only* with friends. Some of my partners are my best friends, and some of my best friends are my partners. I wouldn't have it any other way. When you do business with friends, you will want to follow my father's principle: "Let your financial partners share in the upside as well as mitigate the downside. You *must* share risk fairly."

NEVER SELL INVESTMENT
REAL ESTATE; TRADE IT

JIM GILLESPIE

Jim Gillespie is president and CEO of Coldwell
Banker Real Estate Corporation.

The best real estate advice I ever received came from my
first broker, Bob Dixon at Dixon Gallery of Homes in
LaGrange, Illinois. He told me that "you never sell investment real estate; you trade it."

While a student at the University of Illinois, I realized I
wanted to be in a profession that helped people. My first
jobs were as a schoolteacher and then as a YMCA director
in LaGrange, Illinois. One of my tennis partners was in real
estate, and he convinced me that my personality and work
ethic were perfect for real estate—and, he said, I could also
help people. He was right.

I was thirty years old when Bob imparted this advice,
and I quickly learned that investing in real estate was a very
wise move. Without a lot of money, I made the decision to

buy one home a year and rent it out. The rental income served as a dividend, so to speak, but even at an early age, I focused more on the home appreciation. I came to understand the tax advantages of home ownership, implications of depreciation, and the opportunity to use the homes as leverage in borrowing money.

I have never had trouble finding tenants. I keep my rental prices reasonable, and I keep the properties in excellent shape. I do not regard the rental income as important in the long-term investment strategy. To me, the long-term tax advantages and appreciation make real estate the best investment.

Because of what Bob told me, I never sold a home without buying another. I moved up in quality of homes and locations. I have taken advantage of the Starker 1031 Tax-Free Exchange, which allows you to trade like-kind investment properties with limited or no tax consequences. (But always check with your tax adviser.) My rental income will fund the vast majority of my retirement.

I feel blessed that my tennis partner got me into real estate. I have met many fascinating people and made wonderful friends along the way. Best of all, I met my wife through the business. I have spent thirty of my thirty-one years in real estate connected to the Coldwell Banker organization. I am biased, but I believe that this organization is the greatest real estate organization in the world.

PAY ATTENTION TO DETAILS

LEWIS M. GOODKIN

Lewis M. Goodkin, CEO of Goodkin Consulting Corporation,
is one of the nation's leading consultants to the real estate
industry, a frequent lecturer on urban land economics,
real estate investment, development and marketing,
and the author of *When Real Estate and Home Building
Become Big Business* and more than one thousand
articles for the trade, business associations,
newspapers, and magazines.

I have found that the vast majority of players in this exciting industry called real estate often ignore some of the most basic advice. Clients who pay close attention to details often make better decisions and come up with superior projects. You may make more money than you will ever need, but you should never stop yearning for knowledge in the ever-changing world of real estate. Here are three important ways to be sure you are paying attention to the right details:

1. We sell and rent real estate products to people, not statistics, and the more knowledgeable you are about the people who make up your market(s), the more successful you will be in satisfying their wants, needs, and abilities.

2. In real estate, we often observe that amateurs fail because they miss the subtleties of the market while experts fail because they miss the obvious.

3. The most successful real estate projects result from developers paying attention to the hundreds of little details that are overlooked by their competition but greatly appreciated by their target market(s).

MANAGE YOUR **34** TAX PAYMENTS

GARY GORMAN

Gary Gorman is founder and managing partner of 1031
Exchange Experts, LLC, a real estate tax specialist,
and author of *Exchanging UP!*

W hen you sell real estate, pay tax only *if* you want, *when* you want, and *in the amount* you decide. I learned this valuable lesson more than twenty years ago when I was a tax manager in the San Francisco office of Price Waterhouse & Co. (now PricewaterhouseCooper). At that time I had a client who was buying and selling real estate and deferring the taxes on the profits from the sales by doing 1031 Exchanges. IRS Code Section 1031 lets taxpayers roll the gain from the sale of their old investment property over to their new investment property; therefore, they do not have to pay capital gains tax on the increase at that time. This is one of the tremendous advantages of owning real estate over owning stocks and bonds because there is no comparable code section for stocks and bonds.

Little did I know that my work with this client would be the start of a great career and would lead me to building a substantial fortune of my own in real estate. After 1991, when the IRS changed the rules for 1031 Exchanges and started requiring qualified intermediaries on every exchange, I felt myself being pulled back into the 1031 arena. Capitalizing on my background in real estate and my skills as a CPA, I soon retired from my CPA practice and set up business as a qualified intermediary. This intermediary business has handled in excess of forty thousand exchange transactions since then.

Experience has taught me that regardless of the size or complexity of the transaction, every exchange must have six basic components to successfully defer the taxes:

1. *Hold property for investment.* Both the old property you are selling and the new property you are buying must be held for *investment.* Any type of property qualifies as long as it is investment property. You can sell a purple duplex and buy an office building, an apartment building, a warehouse, or even bare land. Properties held briefly, such as fix-and-flips, don't qualify for exchanges. In general, you have to hold the old property and the new property as investments for at least a year and a day.

Anything that is classified as "real estate" qualifies for an exchange. You can use water rights, timber rights, or mineral rights, such as oil and gas interests, in an exchange.

Vacation homes and second homes have become popular 1031 properties in the last few years.

2. *Limit your properties to three or less.* From the day you close the sale of your old property, you have forty-five days to provide your intermediary with a list of properties you might like to buy. Typically your list will contain three properties or less, and the forty-five days are calendar days. No extensions will be allowed just because the date falls on a weekend or a holiday.

There are no limitations on the properties if your list contains three properties or less. For example, you could sell your purple duplex for $100,000 and list three properties for $10 million each (a total of $30 million), and this is okay. But if you list more than three properties, your total list cannot be more than twice the selling price of your old property. If we change our example and instead list four properties for $75,000 each (a total of only $300,000), your entire exchange is toast—meaning that your whole exchange fails (even if you bought only one of the properties) because you listed more than three properties *and* your list exceeded twice the selling price of your purple duplex. The rule of thumb here is to keep it simple and limit your list to three properties or less.

Your identifications must be clear enough that if the IRS audits you, the agents can go directly to each property to verify the list. Cite "123 Main Street, Denver, Colorado," for example, rather than "a three-bedroom, two-bath house on Main Street, Denver, Colorado." Use a legal description for bare land that doesn't have a mailing address.

Your list must be in the hands of your intermediary before midnight on the forty-fifth day. You can mail it, fax it, or hand-deliver it, but the intermediary must have it by that date. After midnight of the forty-fifth day no changes are allowed to the list, and severe penalties, including prison terms, can be imposed if the IRS finds that you altered it.

3. *Close on new property within 180 days.* From the day you close on the sale of your old property you have 180 days to close on the purchase of your new property, and whatever property you purchase has to be on your forty-five-day list. You could buy one or all three of the properties on the list. Like the forty-five-day requirement, the 180 days are calendar days (including weekends and holidays), and there are no extensions.

Purchasing the property means that you have to take title to the property and the title has to be in your name before the 180th day. You need to close the week before if your 180th day falls on a Saturday, Sunday, or holiday. We always become nervous when our clients take the closing right down to the last minute.

4. *Choose a qualified intermediary.* You cannot touch the money between the sale of your old property and the purchase of your new property. The law requires that you use an independent third party called a qualified intermediary to

hold this money for you. Be careful in choosing a qualified intermediary because the law doesn't protect you from a disreputable intermediary. A recent court case held that if your money is not in a separate account just for you, it is available to any creditor of the intermediary. Make sure that your intermediary puts your money in a separate account for you!

You would think, with such an important role in the exchange process, that federal or state laws would be on the books to protect you and your money from unscrupulous intermediaries. But there are no such laws—nobody is protecting you.

5. *Recognize that titleholders of the old property and the new property must be the same.* The tax return that holds title to the old property is the tax return that must take title to the new property. For example, if Fred and Sue Jones sold their purple duplex, then Fred and Sue have to take title to the new property. They can't take title as Jones Investment Corporation because the corporation is a different taxpayer.

Corporations, partnerships, limited liability companies (LLCs), and trusts can also do 1031 Exchanges. However, these ownership vehicles can make an exchange complicated. For example, if you hold title to your property in a partnership and the partners want to go different directions after the sale, the structure of the exchange will need close guidance from your intermediary, so make sure that you are working with a qualified one.

6. *Buy something of equal or greater value.* To avoid paying any tax at the time of the exchange, you have to buy property of equal or greater value and reinvest all of the cash. For example, if Fred and Sue sell their duplex for $100,000, they have to buy their new property for at least $100,000 to avoid paying taxes. If they pay only $90,000 for the new property, they will pay tax on the $10,000 buy-down. If they sold the duplex and paid off the mortgage and closing costs totaling $40,000, meaning that the balance of $60,000 went to their intermediary, they would have to reinvest all of the $60,000. If they bought their new property for $150,000 and paid for it by getting a new mortgage of $100,000 but used only $50,000 of the $60,000 that the intermediary is holding, they would have to pay tax on the unspent balance of $10,000. (Notice I did not say that in order to qualify for a 1031 Exchange, they would have to secure a loan on the new property at least equal to the loan that was paid off on the old property. This is not a requirement, although many tax and exchange advisers seem to think so.)

There is no limit to the number of exchanges you can do, and you can continue to roll your gains from one property to another until you decide to take some portion of the proceeds at the time of sale, at which point you will incur tax. In this way you control the amount of cash from the transaction that will become taxable. Refinancing the new property is a popular way of accessing cash with no tax liability.

ALWAYS NEGOTIATE

GEORGE E. GRACE

George E. Grace is founder of G. E. Grace & Company, Inc.,
and a member of the Real Estate Board of New York.
He served as a consultant with the company that
pioneered tenant representation in New York City.

G. E. Grace & Company, Inc., represents corporate tenants leasing commercial space. An old-timer, with whom I trained, gave me some advice that has proven valuable again and again. However, like many simple yet sage words, it took five minutes to learn and a lifetime to master.

The advice: always negotiate among several viable options.

When you have more than one landlord competing for your tenancy, you can favorably enhance the economic outcome of a deal.

Sellers in general—landlords and their agents in particular—are in a competitive marketplace. They do not like losing a tenant to a rival or having their building empty.

They do not want to lose the deal. The more you make landlords compete, the more they want to win, and that's when you and your client achieve the best results.

This advice has saved our clients millions of dollars through lower rents, larger concession packages, and more favorable lease terms. The advice underlies almost every negotiation we undertake.

There are many corollaries to this advice. Tenants frequently limit their options. Do not let them. Find additional alternatives. If you do not have any viable option, do not overplay your hand. When you have a great deal, stop negotiating and take it.

BELIEVE IN THE MARKET

38

HARVEY E. GREEN

Harvey E. Green is president and CEO of Marcus & Millichap Real Estate Investment Brokerage Company, one of the largest investment real estate brokerage firms in the United States.

As a young man, just out of the army, I began my real estate career almost by accident, or because I lacked other inspiring career choices.

I entered the business as a striving broker, as a result of great mentoring I received from my brother-in-law, who was a father figure and a person whose business and life experiences I respected. His initial good advice of getting into the industry as a broker was quickly overshadowed by what he told me shortly afterward. The best advice he gave me was simply to be in the real estate market as an investor and to believe in the market.

He clearly understood that throughout time, real estate has endured as one of the most effective, if not *the* most effective, vehicles for creating wealth and security over the long term. Regardless of cycles and temporary gyrations, real estate values have always increased over time, and income returns have been extremely competitive, especially on a risk-adjusted basis.

As for the specific advice and lessons learned, they cover five main areas related to real estate investing:

1. *Know who you are as an investor.* Know why you are investing in each specific property, what your goals are within a set time frame for each individual investment, and what your exit strategy is before you even make an offer.

2. *Assemble the right team.* Even as an individual investor, you need a team of experts on your side who are smarter and better than you in their own respective fields of expertise. Bring together a professional broker, a mortgage broker, an experienced due diligence source, a skilled real estate attorney, a professional property manager, an expert real estate accountant, and a tax expert as a team, no matter what.

3. *Approach acquisitions the way the professionals do.* The real profit is made when real estate is bought, not when it's sold. You need to have a specific value creation strategy for each property, whether that value will be found in operating the real estate in an optimal fashion or whether renovation and/or repositioning can lead to a higher value. Approach due diligence systematically, like a preflight checklist, because to buy on the fly is to hope to get lucky.

4. *Recognize that barriers to entry are more important than location alone.* Location undoubtedly helps drive value, but more than that, a supply-constrained area where people want to be helps lock in better returns during the ownership and long-term value. Supply limitations can be geographical, political, or both and function as a natural break against future competition.

5. *Think long-term, but act on short-term opportunities.* Real estate is forgiving over time and can bury mistakes, but those mistakes can be very painful if you are forced to sell at a specific time. An overextended investor without diversity will also suffer when incomes turn down. Leveraging the market through ups and downs requires long-term patience. A long-term view usually pays off. However, astute investors are keenly aware of the fact that for every property, there is a time to sell. Measuring diminishing return on equity and the opportunity cost of locking in too much in one or a few properties will limit the upside and increase risk in many cases. As an investor, you should always look for investment opportunity, regardless of the cycle.

ALWAYS HONOR YOUR DEALS

JEFFREY GURAL

Jeffrey Gural is chairman of Newmark & Company Real Estate, Inc., one of the largest independent real estate service firms in the world. He also serves on the board of directors of the Real Estate Board of New York.

Twenty-five years ago I shook hands with an elderly gentleman named Sam Galewitz to purchase a group of buildings on Broadway and Astor Place for $9 million. A few days later, I heard through the grapevine that Sam had received an offer of $10 million from an acquaintance of mine who was unaware that I was in on the deal. I thought for sure I would lose the deal, and sure enough Sam called to say he was offered $1 million more than I had offered. I expected him to either say he was sorry or give me the opportunity to match the higher offer. To my surprise, he simply said that he would honor his handshake provided I would promise not to make him look like a fool and flip the contract for the $1 million profit. He explained that his

102

father told him that you should never go back on your word and that his handshake was as good as a written agreement.

I've always remembered Sam and his father's advice, and I've never, in more than twenty-five years, reneged on a deal. I believe that has served me well because brokers will always bring tenants to the buildings we own because we can be relied on to keep our word once a deal is brokered. Incredibly, we still own the building we bought from Sam years ago, and today it is probably worth well over $100 million.

TODOAY'S RENTER IS TOMORROW'S BUYER

ANDREW HEIBERGER

Andrew Heiberger is president and CEO of Buttonwood Real Estate LLC, a Manhattan-based real estate company focusing on development, investment, and syndication. He is also the founder and former CEO of Citi Habitats, Inc., one of New York City's largest and most successful residential real estate brokerages.

My father and mother were active in the Long Island real estate market, and I was captivated by the industry at an early age. By the time I got to Manhattan at the age of twenty-two, there were plenty of ambitious ideas swimming around my head. Back then, however, there were not a lot of schools serving as pipelines into the real estate world. In fact, there were a very limited number of ways for young people to get into the industry. You could come in as a property manager, or, if you were lucky, you could make coffee and run errands for a developer. One field that was particularly closed to young professionals was the residential brokerage business. Most people thought that if your hair wasn't gray and your name wasn't Gladys, you had no business selling apartments in Manhattan.

Moreover, rentals had long been neglected in the brokerage business because of the lower commissions commonly associated with them. This neglect was utterly puzzling to me because most people who come to New York choose to rent, and anyone who has done it knows it isn't easy. Who wouldn't want a friendly face showing them around an unfamiliar big city? I decided to be that friendly face.

After some initial success finding apartments for people, I started Citi Habitats, Inc. My goal was to create Manhattan's predominant residential brokerage through capturing the market of young renters. By developing a relationship with first-time renters, I knew I could set myself up for repeat business. The way I saw it, today's $1,500 rental could be tomorrow's $2 million purchase.

The key was to build bonds with clients and hold on relentlessly. It meant treating real estate as a true service industry. The first step was to be polite and grateful to clients, regardless of whether they decided to rent from me. This might sound obvious, but brokers had developed a deservedly negative reputation. Generosity and a smile go a long way in a service industry.

The second step was to spread goodwill beyond the client base—the renters. Landlords, doormen, and receptionists needed to be part of my team. While each required a different kind of attention, all were equally important. I instituted a methodical system to maintain contact with them. When these relationships gave me an inside track on a vacancy, I knew the listing was mine.

Next, I set out to ensure that no client ever got away. Even after a deal was closed, I did not let up. Part of this strategy involved creating separate businesses within our organization that maintained contact with our client and customer bases. For customers, programs such as our concierge and relocation services guaranteed that we remained relevant and useful long after they had signed a lease. For landlords and developers, regular market reports and on-site marketing services made us a valuable resource. My goal was to remain important to all clients and customers. I also knew that today's customer was tomorrow's referral. This model had never been properly executed before, and I was determined to make it work. A willingness to take chances and to try new things is essential for any real estate entrepreneur.

The key to making this model work was a proactive and effective organizational system with a detailed database filled with thousands of names. Past clients, friends of clients, and those who opted not to be clients heard from us regularly. There was no reason why a client should not be a repeat customer or a valuable referral. Citi Habitats grew to twenty offices throughout Manhattan, with more than one thousand employees, and became the industry leader in Web site technology. Though some of my company's marketing techniques were cutting edge and unconventional, they were vital to distinguishing Citi Habitats from its competition. As a result, Citi Habitats became Manhattan's preeminent residential real estate brokerage—the goal I had set for it.

OPPORTUNITIES ALWAYS EXIST

DOROTHY HERMAN

Dorothy Herman is president and CEO of
Prudential Douglas Elliman, the largest and fastest-
growing real estate firm in New York City.

started my career in the early 1980s. The first day on the job, I met with my boss for orientation. After assuring me of how well he thought I would do, he gave me some advice that I would never forget. "This is a job," he said, "and jobs help you make a living. If you want to build wealth and create financial freedom, you can't just sell real estate; you need to invest in it personally. Most of the self-made millionaires in this country made their money in real estate. You should start now."

I replied, "The interest rates are at 18 percent; it's not a good time."

He said, "There is never a wrong time to buy real estate. When times are good, people complain about the deals they have missed. When times are bad, they claim they can't buy at the top thinking that prices will fall and, therefore, it's not a good investment."

The lesson I have learned is that you can build wealth in any real estate market, good or bad. The only constant is change. When the market changes, it brings new and different opportunities. You just have to be on the lookout for them. There is never a bad time to buy as long as you choose the right strategy.

Twenty-five years later, I give people that same advice. It still holds true.

LEAVE BOTH PARTIES HAPPY

THOMAS J. HUTCHISON III

Thomas J. Hutchison is CEO of CNL Hotels & Resorts, Inc.,
one of the nation's largest real estate investment
trusts in the lodging industry.

The best real estate deal is the deal that you walk away from with the feeling that both parties achieved what they wanted. All principals in a deal must be winners; all sides must truly feel that they prevailed. This is the artistry and the fun of the deal, the Rembrandt that sparks years of repeat business transactions and enduring long-term relationships grounded in mutual respect, trust, and integrity.

Why is this so critical to real estate transactions? How can you fully anticipate the demands of the other side?

At the end of the day, I like to feel good about the transaction we have consummated. If you try to steal real estate as a buyer, the seller loses. If you ask too much, you may lose by never selling. You have to consistently strike a balance to be successful in this business—take a step back, slow down, take in the big picture—whatever you need to do to ignite your own critical thinking discipline. For me, that equates to:

- intensely questioning the situation
- analyzing and internalizing the options
- formulating reasoned judgments and resulting objectives
- reflecting on the strategy of persuasion, evaluating the needs from both ends of the transaction
- surrounding myself with the brightest people in the business

And when the occasion presents itself, I do not hesitate to excuse myself from the table to grab a cup of coffee or take a walk to allow further internal reflection and thought. Decisions are the lifeblood of real estate, and you want to ensure they evoke the critical thought that reaps rewards for your business and its future.

You have to train yourself to be a great listener, evaluate your first reaction, challenge your intellectual strength, and above all, trust your conscience. When I listen to my executives or my business partners, I intently listen with three things: my brain, my heart, and my gut. The hard part is to understand which of these impulses, or combination, is ultimately driving my decisions. Doing this requires experienced discernment.

Over the past several years, some of my company's most pivotal and profitable transactions have been initiated by a phone call and dinner among friends. The most compelling real estate assets are not always marketed, as several of my company's acquisitions prove. In fact, many real estate owners will entertain offers only from someone they know will play fair and will do what he or she said the first time. Again, this comes from years and years of maintaining great win-win relationships.

When you can have a casual dinner at a resort with your wife and say to her, "I think we should buy this property someday," and make it a reality several months later prior to its being placed on the market, that's the underlying strength of a great business relationship.

How does one go about fostering and strengthening relationships in the real estate industry? From your very first day on the job, you must assume that each and every person you interface with has the potential to become one of the biggest assets in your career. This business is organically developed, it's cyclical, it's multigenerational, and you cannot have too many people in your corner. Network with your allies and your major competitors; there should not be a distinction between them. Knowing more about your competition will often result in a higher rate of success in achieving your goals.

Relationships do not always come easily; obviously it takes work from both sides. Once, in my early career, I asked my assistant to book me a first-class seat next to the CEO of an interior design firm whom I really wanted to meet. The three-hour flight was the beginning of a thirty-year relationship, and incidentally my company at the time received a large contract from his firm as a result.

After almost thirty-five years in real estate, I reflect fondly on the fair and honest dealings that have transpired and the wealth that has been produced on both sides of the table. The common denominator is clearly the intangible power of enduring relationships, not the fierce desire to always win big.

GET INTO THE COMMERCIAL
REAL ESTATE BUSINESS

THOMAS J. HYNES JR.

Thomas Hynes is president of Meredith & Grew, a full-service
commercial real estate firm headquartered in Boston.

The best advice I ever received about the real estate business was simple and straightforward: "Go into the commercial real estate business. Boston has a great future, and
you should be part of it." My uncle, John B. Hynes, who was
then mayor of Boston, spoke those words to me many times.

Our family was steeped in Boston politics since my
uncle was the city's mayor from 1949 to 1960. I graduated
from Boston College in 1961 and entered the U.S. Army as
a second lieutenant. When I came home on leave, I visited
my uncle to ask for career advice.

As mayor, John B. Hynes brought the Prudential
Insurance Company to the city, and that company built
the first major office complex in Boston following the
Depression. He commented that, for his efforts, he was

114

paid his annual salary of $20,000 a year as he watched Jack Fallon, a young broker from R. M. Bradley, make millions as leasing and managing agent for the complex.

My uncle noted that unless you graduated from the top of your class at Harvard Law School, you could not get into any of the major law firms in Boston, and many young lawyers were barely eking out a living. Unless you were independently wealthy, a career in politics created a very difficult financial strain to raise a family. However, the real estate market had great upside potential.

I finished my tour of duty in the army and entered law school. After completing the first year, I was back to my old summer job of wrecking buildings since there were no law firm internships available and I needed to pay for the next year's tuition. While working in demolition, which was an extremely dangerous job, I began to think daily about jump-starting my political career and running for office. With the income from the legislative salary to finance my law school education, my political career would be off and running.

I had about a week to make up my mind and start a campaign when one of my coworkers, standing ten feet away from me, was killed on the job. The next day I put on a suit and went to my uncle's office to inform him that I was going to run for the office of the Great and General Court of Massachusetts. He quietly gave his opinion that I would lose the election because I was running against a first-term incumbent. "Remember what I said about the real estate business," he told me as he wrote out a $100 check for my campaign.

We ran a great campaign and I finished runner-up out of thirteen candidates, but I lost and was faced with the campaign debt and the reality of not going back to law school. "What do you think of the real estate business now?" my uncle asked. My response was, "I think it's a great idea. How do I start?" The first person he said I should call was Jack Fallon, whom he had used as a role model. I met Jack and quickly found he was all that my uncle had described—a big, handsome, gregarious guy who made millions in the real estate business . . . a classic power broker of the 1960s. I had my heart set on working for him, but he never called me back.

My uncle called another friend, Tom Horan of Meredith & Grew, who had built the Travelers Insurance complex in Boston. After meeting Mr. Horan, I was convinced that Meredith & Grew was the place for me. However, Mr. Horan's partner asked me what I knew about the real estate business besides knocking buildings down—not exactly a warm welcome. Weeks went by, again with no returned calls. I continued networking and then made one last desperate call to Meredith & Grew, which got me back in the door and a job. I have been at Meredith & Grew since 1965 and have been ever grateful for the opportunities at the firm and in the business.

By the way, my political experience was a great training ground because I had knocked on hundreds of doors asking for votes. How simple was it to knock on doors and ask people if they wanted help with their real estate needs? Another element of politics is meeting people at every stage of life, which has many parallels in the real estate business.

I am eternally grateful for the guidance and wisdom of my uncle, Mayor John B. Hynes, who steered me in the right direction and was instrumental in my real estate career. Along the way I learned to recognize when it's time to change course and when it's time to persevere, and I learned not to be afraid to take risks.

Clearly my uncle gave me the best advice I ever received.

NEVER SHOW EMOTION;
BE PATIENT; WORK HARD;
AND CREATE VOLUME

EREZ ITZHAKI

Erez Itzhaki is founder and CEO of Itzhaki Properties NY, Inc.,
a full-service real estate brokerage firm. He formerly
managed his own real estate firm in Israel.

The first rule in real estate is to never, *ever* show emotion.
Obviously there's no future in expressing disappointment or anger, but I believe there is just as much danger in showing excitement. Insecurity of any sort, expressed or unexpressed, erodes success. The same is true of assuming that anyone in a transaction is superior to another. Every deal, big or small, is based on numbers, as I see it, and transactions are simply articulations of those numbers when all players are treated equally.

It's easy to see why emotion doesn't fit when you deal from a position that is unfailingly honest. Shortcuts are inappropriate. Honesty and creativity are crucial because at the end of the day the real estate business is sustained by the network you create and the reputation you earn.

Another position that I've taken—and obviously not everyone does this—has to do with timing. I'm not particularly interested in being a pioneer. Yes, there are people and companies who've done quite well by seeing what's happening, figuring out where the next growth will be, and acting on that vision. The individuals who bought property near the World Trade Center after 9/11 are a perfect example of what happens when one has the right intuition.

In my estimation, though, the better move is to follow the leader. For example, in commercial real estate, I like to wait until high-end retail outlets move in. That is the harbinger of the "second cycle," where the returns can be particularly handsome. And, of course, acting promptly is just as important as waiting to move. I try to be neither the first nor the last.

If I have a child who wishes to go into real estate (my wife is expecting as I write this), my advice would be pretty simple: patience, patience, patience. Work hard—seven days a week—and create volume because you can expect only one opportunity out of ten to come through. At the end of the day, though, be content to wait, wait, wait. That, I guess, is why emotion is so deadly and honesty is so important.

KNOW WHEN TO
ANTICIPATE OPPORTUNITIES

CHARLES JACOBUS

Charles Jacobus is an author, educator, title insurance executive, and board-certified real estate lawyer from Houston, Texas.

When the amateurs start getting into the area of real estate in which you work or invest, you should know that it's time to get out.

Successful real estate investors profit significantly from experience. The bad experiences help you appreciate the good ones, and that process doesn't happen overnight. When real estate investing begins to look easy and profitable, everyone thinks he can invest without regard to traditional, time-tested objectives and strategies. Amateur investors, looking for the easy buck, often outbid the real market because "everything is going up," they do very little real analysis, and they have no exit strategy. When a number of amateur investors buy too high, it creates a false market that is too high. The amateurs usually do not have cash flow, which sets up a downfall, or "crash," one sees in the cyclical real estate market. When the crash occurs, the idealists sell off in a bad market at a loss. The experienced real estate investors step in again and buy cheap, and the project can cash-flow at the lower purchase price. When the amateurs get in, it's time to wait for the opportunity you know is coming.

WORK TO GET A GOOD DEAL

OZZIE JUROCK

Ozzie Jurock writes about, teaches, and buys and sells
real estate. He is a real estate columnist for the *Vancouver Sun*
and *Business in Vancouver* and author of *Forget About Location,
Location, Location*. *Vancouver* magazine ranked him
among the forty-five brightest people in Vancouver,
British Columbia, Canada.

The best real estate advice I ever received was from my
first branch manager in 1968: "For the individual, there
is no such thing as a good market or a bad market, only
whether or not he or she has a good or a bad deal."

People always want to know whether it is a good market or a bad market. For thirty-five years I have listened to
talk about bubbles, hot markets, seller's markets, and
buyer's markets. But you know what? No matter what the
market, ownership of the average home outperforms any
other investment.

THE BEST REAL ESTATE ADVICE I EVER RECEIVED

KNOW WHO YOU ARE

To be successful in real estate, you need to find the good deals, have the guts to act, and know who *you* are. Are you a Shark, a Flipper, or an Investor?

Do you want to

- make the quick deal, quick profit?
- build a long-term portfolio?
- create long-term passive income?

The *Shark* is a grave danger. He benefits from the misery of others. The Shark will always be able to find someone, whether in good times or bad, who needs to sell quickly and cheaply because of an illness, a death, a divorce, a job transfer, a business reversal, the loss of a job, bankruptcy, or because someone got too greedy, too sleepy, or too stupid. Bad times simply make the soup a little thicker, but such sellers are always there. If you want to deal in foreclosures, auctions, and tough deals, you have to sit in court. Evaluate. Learn about how to buy cheaply and wisely.

The *Flipper* works on the other side of the scale. For him, the good times with a rising market and rapidly rising inflation give him the most opportunities. But even in a flat market with no inflation, he can find deals; he just has to work a little harder and wait a little longer for them.

There is a tendency in a rising, inflationary market to

jump on the conveyor belt at any price because of the "bigger fool theory"—a bigger fool will come along and buy your property and give you a profit. This is fine as long as you are not the last fool in line.

Yes, you can be both a Shark and a Flipper. The Shark and the Flipper need to have the ability to recognize the signs, interpret them correctly, and then act without hesitation. But remember that the Shark and the Flipper don't deal in averages. They deal in *exceptions!*

If you want to be a Shark or a Flipper, you have to ask yourself where you draw the line between morals and business because the Shark prospers from someone else's misery and the Flipper takes advantage of someone else's ignorance to deprive him of potential profit. Everyone has to decide on the morals of the situation for himself or herself.

The *Investor* is primarily concerned with finding low-down-payment, cash-flowing property using personal rules (e.g., the 1 percent rule—the monthly payments of 1 percent of the purchase price will service a 100 percent financed property and cash flow). The Investor looks for safety and quality tenants to create a passive income stream sometime in the future. For instance, the Investor may buy five condominiums at, say, $80,000 each, with an $800 per month income and nothing down. After owning them for eighteen years, the Investor will have an income of $4,000 per month forever ($4,000 will service $1 million).

The Shark and the Flipper buy anywhere. They are in and out of the deal within three to six months. The Investor *must* buy where the ratio of rental income is in line with the price he pays. The Investor looks for a good working environment such as a suburb or a smaller town. Investors generally outperform Sharks and Flippers over time.

The bad news? Whether you decide you are a Shark, a Flipper, or an Investor, you have to do some work! No guru, no Realtor, no "market" is going to find you the great deal. *You* must do it yourself. The market is irrelevant. Your commitment to learning and growing is everything.

Know Your Local Market

Some other points worth remembering are these:

- Real estate markets—unlike stock markets—are local in nature. Gold sales last night in Hong Kong affect gold prices in New York today. Real estate market changes in Hong Kong don't mean beans in San Francisco. Understand your local market.
- It is not location, location, location. Real estate is local and cyclical. You could have bought in the greatest location in New York, San Diego, and a thousand other places in the late '80s and lost your shirt. You could have bought anything anywhere and made a fortune in the last four years in the same locations.

Location for the average person is not nearly as important as knowing how long the cycles have run and what stage the local cycle is in.

- You make the most money on the day you buy. No matter what the market, you will always make the most money because of your due diligence, your astute assessment, and your guts to act.

- In the end, the quality of your life is determined not by how much you understand and know, but by the actions you take.

TAKE CAREFUL RISKS AND HAVE FUN

BRUCE KARATZ

Bruce Karatz is chairman and CEO of KB Home, one of the largest homebuilders in the United States and France, which was recently named the #1 Homebuilder on *Fortune* magazine's list of America's "Most Admired Companies."

When I was asked as a young executive to go to Paris and take over KB Home's operations in France, the local office manager, who knew I didn't speak a word of French, naturally assumed I'd want an English-speaking assistant who would also translate for me.

It was a tempting offer and certainly would have been the easy, comfortable choice. But in business—and in real estate—it's often more important to make choices that make you uncomfortable. So with some anxiety, I turned down the translator. And while it was incredibly frustrating at times, I ultimately became a better leader for it. If you stay in your comfort zone, you'll never be in a position to make bold bets, which ultimately define who you are and how far you will go.

A BUSINESS MODEL

There's a right way and a wrong way to take business risks. Real estate is a risky enough game; you don't need to turn it into a sheer gamble. The right way is to have a basic framework in place—a business model—to guide your decision making. A great business model is really a growth engine. We developed our model (which we call "KBnxt") over the course of several years, and it has been a remarkably durable guide that has helped us successfully navigate the housing market.

Our business model gave me the confidence to make a risky bet about the scale of our operations. In the 1990s, conventional wisdom said that no one builder could construct more than twenty thousand homes in a single year. It was thought to be just too much of a management and logistical stretch, and a builder's internal processes couldn't handle it.

I challenged that thinking by expanding aggressively and found that not only could we get the traditional benefits of scale—better and less expensive access to labor and materials—but we could do things for our customers that we could not do as a smaller builder. Chief among them, we were able to offer buyers an unprecedented number of choices, giving them a true custom-home experience. Today, maximizing customer choice is considered obvious, but it wasn't too long ago that it was considered a pretty radical idea for the homebuilding industry.

In spite of that "conventional wisdom," KB Home is now constructing almost forty thousand homes a year—while offering more custom choices to buyers than ever before.

A MARKETING PLAN

I also made risky bets on marketing. Few homebuilders had ever tried to develop a locally recognizable brand—let alone a nationally recognized one—but I thought that building a brand was as important to a homebuilder as it was to any other consumer product. So we set out to launch high-profile promotions, which included building a full-size home on the back lot of the *Regis & Kelly* show in the heart of Manhattan; creating a real-life version of *The Simpsons'* house in Las Vegas; and most recently partnering with Martha Stewart to build homes and communities based on her unique design sensibility. KB Home is now the most recognized brand in homebuilding, with buyers naming us nearly four times more than our next five competitors combined.

A GREAT TEAM

Having a great team makes all this possible. That's why I don't take risks on the quality of our employees. I try to hire the best and invest heavily in keeping their skills up to date. The more than 6,500 people of KB Home are connected by the passion we have to build a great business and the fun we have every day too. After all, it's fun to take risks. It's fun to grow. It's fun to make a name for yourself and to break free from the pack.

And when you love what you do for a living, you never really "work" a day in your life.

CAPTURE THE BUYER'S IMAGINATION

48

CRAIG KING

Craig King is president of J. P. King Auction Company,
the nation's most successful auction company
marketing luxury real estate.

The advice came from my father, J. P. King: sell dreams,
not dirt.

Dirt is cheap, but dreams are priceless. If you're selling
land, focus on what the property can be—such as a business, a home, a shopping center, a retreat. Capture a man's
imagination, and he'll not only pay top dollar, but thank
you for the privilege.

PROTECT YOUR CLIENTS FROM THEMSELVES

MICHELE KLEIER

Michele Kleier is president of Gumley Haft Kleier, one of
the ten largest residential brokerage firms in Manhattan.

When I was new in the business, I had been working with a client for many months. She had quite a few "must haves," including a washer and dryer, views, and a doorman. Her absolute nonnegotiable must, however, was "I must be below Eightieth Street." Well, after all that time together, I finally found the perfect apartment for her. Large eat-in kitchen with a washer and dryer, a high floor facing Park Avenue with views, a wood-burning fireplace . . . there was only one problem. It was ten blocks north of her cutoff. I begged her to see it, and she refused every time. I listened.

Another broker did not. This broker made an appointment at an apartment on Park and Ninetieth Street but didn't tell the client where she was going. Six months later, the client was signed, sealed, and delivered onto the building's doorstep in the very location she swore she would never step foot in. You can imagine the mortification for both of us, especially since the Park and Ninetieth Street apartment she bought was in my building!

Well, the buyer felt so guilty, she referred me to everyone she knew, and we became great friends. Years later, when she finally decided to move to the Hamptons, she gave me the exclusive on her apartment, which I sold to a client for just under $3 million. The buyer had originally paid only $250,000 for it! Four short years later, the apartment once again paid off, this time for me. I just resold it for $6 million.

Just as men often marry brunettes after years of dating only blondes, and end up strolling on Madison Avenue with the small white puppy they swore they would never have, buyers are liars. Only they don't know it. People who want only prewar structures are often the first ones to sign a contract in new construction; people who feel they are the epitome of the Upper West Side wind up gazing from their new living rooms onto the East River; and Tribeca loft dwellers often end up with Fifth Avenue addresses.

If you're a great broker, you very often know your customers' tastes better than they know them. Sometimes, you just have to use your intuition and say, "Trust me."

PICK AN AREA OF SPECIALIZATION

ROBERT A. KNAKAL

Robert A. Knakal is chairman and founding partner
of Massey Knakal Realty Services, a real estate
brokerage firm specializing in investment property sales
throughout New York City and the surrounding
New York metropolitan area.

The best real estate advice I ever received was to pick an area of specialization and to stay true to it by becoming the very best within that discipline. Doing this has enabled my firm to achieve four distinct benefits:

1. Superior market knowledge
2. A tremendous competitive advantage
3. The ability to easily differentiate our services
4. The platform to become the best building sales brokerage firm in New York

SPECIALIZE

Massey Knakal's operating model is highly specialized. We sell only properties, we represent sellers on an exclusive basis, and we work within a strict "territory system." We have divided the five boroughs of New York City into eighty-six territories, with one agent working in each neighborhood. New York City is far too big for any one agent to know everything about every area; focusing on one neighborhood makes it possible to achieve a high level of market insight. If a client owns three properties in different neighborhoods, we are able to provide accurate, high-quality market information within minutes from the agents in those territories.

Focusing on one neighborhood or area helps our agents establish a track record much more expeditiously. If agents have been active within their territories for only six or nine months but have sold three properties, their credibility in the local market is significantly higher than someone who may have been active for two years and sold twenty buildings in twenty different neighborhoods.

Another advantage of the territory system is that agents are able to speak more intelligently about a particular market and a particular topic or issue relevant to that territory. The agents know every property that has been sold within the last couple of years, its condition, tenancy, capitalization rate, and so forth. They also become aware of proposed zoning changes and planned new developments. Many of our agents who have been in the business only a year or two are regularly quoted in stories within the major newspapers and trade publications when an article is written about their neighborhood.

During the emerging stage of Massey Knakal's development, we learned that the real estate brokerage business really has much less to do with real estate and more to do with information—specifically, the quality and quantity of the information make it easy to differentiate our services from those of other firms. Specialization allows this differentiation to take place very rapidly. The quality of our information is significantly more accurate and more detailed than that produced by our competitors.

Through excellent market knowledge and the competitive advantages that knowledge creates, Massey Knakal has become the *best* investment property sales firm focusing solely on New York City property sales. In 2005, our firm sold 572 buildings in the New York City marketplace. This number is four times that of our closest competitor! We are a relatively small firm compared with the real estate giants that operate nationally and regionally, but we have been able to amass this market share simply as a result of the specialization that we have adopted and the focus on obtaining insightful and useful information to the benefit of our clients. Our firm is now the biggest seller of investment properties in New York, but that was never our intention. Our intention was always to be the best, but by being the best we have become the biggest (by being the biggest you may not necessarily be the best).

Based on our experience, becoming a specialist is by far the most important part of our model and success. When people ask how they can start buying buildings or what a good strategy might entail, we always suggest that they pick a neighborhood where they would like to own property and get to know that neighborhood better than anyone else. They can do that by walking the streets, talking to owners, attending community board meetings, going to street fairs, and speaking to others engaged in real estate–related activities in that area.

Do Not Speak Negatively about Competitors

Another bit of real estate advice that has been integral to the success of Massey Knakal has been never to speak negatively about the competition. We believe it is a sign of desperation and insecurity. We always focus on our strengths and differentiate our services from those of our competitors without conveying negative messages. If you are truly confident, you can demonstrate why you, rather than a competitor, should get the business.

YOU MAKE YOUR MONEY WHEN YOU BUY REAL ESTATE, NOT WHEN YOU SELL IT

TOM KUNZ

Tom Kunz is president and CEO of the Century 21 network.

My father's friend Mark Welker once told me that you make your money in real estate when you buy it, not when you sell it.

When I was living in Utah, I fondly remember buying one particular house that many people would have considered a lemon. The former tenants of the four-bedroom ranch had done their best to have the place condemned. It was run down with broken windows and in desperate need of repair. Since it was the middle of winter, snow had settled in like an unwelcome houseguest, not just on the lawn but also inside the house.

Still, I saw potential in this house. It had high ceilings and spacious rooms, and it was structurally sound. I also got a great deal on the house. It sold for $28,000 when the market value was around $75,000. I put all my free time into renovations—new windows, carpets, and paint, which totaled about $10,000 of my own money. The words of my father's friend resonated with me. When I bought the house, I paid next to nothing for it. Through hard work and a little vision, in the end, I received much more than I put into this investment.

LEAVE YOUR EMOTIONS AT HOME

LEONARD LAUDER

Leonard Lauder is chairman of The Estée Lauder
Companies, Inc. He is also a charter trustee of the
University of Pennsylvania and chairman of the Whitney
Museum of American Art in New York City.

In 1958, I received the best real estate advice from Lester
Crown, scion of the famous Crown family of Chicago.
Lester was helpful to me as we were finalizing the lease for
our company at 666 Fifth Avenue. He said, "Leonard, if you
ever invest in real estate, promise me that you won't
become emotionally involved with the property." "Why?"
you may ask. Lester knew that if your emotions were
involved, you would likely lose money. He is very wise, and
I have always followed his sage advice.

FIND A NEED AND FILL IT

STEPHEN LEOPOLD

Stephen Leopold is chairman of William B. May International, the oldest name still operating in New York real estate (www.wbmayre.com). He also founded Leopold Property Consultants in Montreal in 1977, one of the largest companies in North America representing tenants only.

I remember eating Raisin Bran at the age of five. There were never enough raisins in it, so I added more raisins. Decades later, the marketing geniuses at Kellogg's figured out that they needed "two scoops of raisins" in their Raisin Bran. I, along with millions of other kids, had known this a quarter century earlier. And I wasn't even in the first grade!

The same kind of common sense applies to real estate consulting and has a lot to do with how I became chairman of William B. May International, Inc., a commercial real estate brokerage in New York with a boutique approach. When I started in the business, it was clear to me that every part of the leasing process in an office building was geared to the advantage of the landlord. Real estate brokers listed a landlord's space and gave the landlord their expertise, even though the landlord was already a real estate expert. The party needing expertise and sophisticated real estate services was the tenant. And so, thirty years ago, I formed a company unique in North America that represented *only* tenants of office space.

In ten years we became a dominant force in the industry with a professional staff of more than one hundred, including eight full-time in-house lease lawyers. We were doing more business than any other broker with Trizec Hahn, then the largest publicly traded real estate company in North America. A magazine article written about me quoted a Trizec senior vice president: "To say that Leopold defended the interests of tenants in their negotiations with landlords would be an understatement. Leopold brought the intellectual equivalent of tanks, artillery, and aircraft carriers to the tenants' side of the table."

This tenant power that I developed first brought me to New York to represent Celanese, now Hoechst Celanese, the company for which 1211 Avenue of the Americas had been built. Originally called the Celanese Building, it is now known as the News Corporation Building (as in Rupert Murdoch).

ACT WHEN AN OPPORTUNITY PRESENTS ITSELF

I represented Celanese in the Murdoch transaction, and during the negotiations, I had occasion to visit a law firm in the World Trade Center. As a Canadian new to New York at the time, I assumed every office complex in North America had a major food court, just as they do in Montreal, Toronto, Calgary, and Vancouver. Naturally this meant that if I was in the largest office complex in the world, I would be about to visit the largest food court in the world. I was salivating at the thought of entering a facility that would make the culinary selections available at Faneuil Hall look like a peewee baseball team in comparison to the New York Yankees. And so I tapped a security guard on the shoulder and asked, "Where is the food court?"

He told me there was none.

I figured he must be new on the job. But to my astonishment, I discovered that he was correct.

No longer five years of age, I used my Raisin Bran theory. Instead of counting on someone else to add the extra raisins, I added my own raisins and leased approximately two acres of space within the World Trade Center to create the world's largest food courts. Financing for the project was secured only six months prior to September 11, 2001, based on an assumed all-in cost of just under $20 million. Soon afterward, the project was valued on a food-only basis at close to $70 million. And alcohol sales—when the food courts turned into evening or weekend bar and entertainment facilities—would add another $70 million. I sold my stake in the project and was settling in to retire in Lake Tahoe, awaiting payments based on initial food and beverage sales. Site preparation had already begun. Then 9/11 came along.

AVOID CONFLICTS OF INTEREST

And so I find myself back in New York staring at a box of Raisin Bran, which once again does not have enough raisins. And yet again people are asking me, "Why hasn't anybody done *this* before?"

Once again, the *this* responds to gaping real estate needs. Something is wrong when tenants take space in a building at the urging and counsel of a real estate broker who works for the same brokerage company that has a pre-existing and ongoing contract to act as that building's marketing and managing agent. Major incentives have been built into the building broker's marketing contract to do everything imaginable to obtain the *absolute best deal* in every single leasing transaction for the landlord. This, folks, is easier to figure out than "two scoops of raisins." Can you imagine a law firm representing both plaintiff and defendant in the same case, in the same courtroom, on the same day? Yet in real estate it is considered normal to represent a tenant's best interests by "negotiating" with a landlord whom the broker is representing all year long.

Utterly preposterous, yet until recently the market for office leasing advisory services in New York conspicuously lacked a high-grade boutique offering that would put an end to this state of affairs. It had no Harry Winston or Rolls-Royce of office leasing, no Allen and Company or Michael Steinhart.

William B. May is the most venerated name in the annals of New York commercial real estate, and the firm has been in business longer than any other New York real estate company. For more than 140 years, it has served many of New York's most prominent leaders. Most important, we have discarded all conflicts of interest by representing only the tenant in office leasing transactions. This matters to a client. Just as a well-managed, single-minded hedge fund nearly always outperforms a run-of-the-mill mutual fund, the right kind of real estate representation quickly reaches the bottom line.

CHOOSE ONE SIDE

Real estate is one of the last great bastions that permit genuine entrepreneurship, so go ahead and put up your shingle. I have just one last piece of counsel, however. You will wish to avoid something that the late, great Senator Sam Ervin always used to talk about. I was reminded of this story recently by Gene Boyce, who was one of the three interviewers in the famous session when the Watergate tapes were discovered. I served with him as an investigator in 1973 on Sam Ervin's Watergate Committee. This happened to one of Senator Ervin's shadier classmates early in his career, when he was fresh out of law school. An older woman who had a legal problem visited Sam's classmate one day in his brand-new office in North Carolina, and she asked his advice. Sam's classmate gave her his advice, and she rose and started to go out of his office. He said, "Wait a minute, ma'am. You owe me five dollars."

"For what?" she asked.

He said, "For my advice."

And she said, "Well, I ain't gonna take it."

Take this advice: if you avoid the ethical swamp that comes with playing both sides of the office leasing street (or both sides of any street in the great republic of business), you'll never run into the equivalent of that woman in Senator Sam Ervin's story.

CAREFULLY CONSIDER
GROWTH POTENTIAL

PAMELA LIEBMAN

Pamela Liebman is president and CEO of The Corcoran Group,
the largest residential real estate firm in New York City. She
serves on the executive committee and board of governors
of the Real Estate Board of New York.

If you're looking for your home, buy with your heart
more than with your head. But if you want an investment, put on your thinking cap.

Buying a home is an emotional decision. Everybody
likes to feel that he is getting a good deal or that the property values will appreciate, but the truth is that most people
buy a home because it uniquely reflects their personality
and their values. In short, they need to live in it. Think
about what makes a home right for you; home buyers
sometimes make the mistake of focusing on home acquisition as an investment and overlook quality-of-life factors
such as proximity to schools, parks, extended family, and

work—all of which are the aspects of daily life that make for a healthy, safe, and comfortable home.

On the other hand, if you are looking to buy as an investment, you need to have a clear idea of your goals. Decide early on if it's a short- or long-term play. Speculators can make money by buying in new condo developments very early and then flipping the units at the first opportunity for a quick profit. If this is what you are striving for, just be sure to take into account all the additional costs of getting in and out of the properties fast. Many times there are hidden fees that an inexperienced player might miss.

If you are in it for the long term, look for areas that have not yet peaked but have great upward potential. In New York City, people made enormous amounts of money by buying early in downtown neighborhoods while they were still more industrial areas. They saw the long-term potential for them to develop into vital and vibrant communities. The artistic and gay communities typically are early trend spotters and excel at mining the potential of up-and-coming neighborhoods. The Meatpacking District, SoHo, and Chelsea are all good examples of places in New York where this has happened.

CONTROL THE INVENTORY

DAVE LINIGER

Dave Liniger is cofounder and chairman of RE/MAX International, an acronym for "real estate maximums," and cofounder of the Wildlife Experience, the Denver-area conservation center.

Simply put, "The company that controls the inventory controls the marketplace."

That statement may be true in many industries, and in the real estate business it is an absolute fact—almost a rule. I received this advice early in my real estate career, and I never forgot it. Now, some forty years later, it's still true. And it is applicable in all areas of real estate—residential housing, luxury properties, commercial real estate, and investment properties.

In this context, the word *control* does not mean "manipulate" values. The reference refers to which real estate firm or company will be the most successful and have the most opportunities to work with the buyers and sellers of real estate. Market value is always determined by negotiated agreements between sellers and buyers. The job of a real estate agent is to assist in those negotiations, but it all starts with a seller deciding to sell a property and choosing a real estate company as a representative for the transaction, through a listing agreement. Interested buyers and their real estate representatives are now aware of the property through an abundance of advertising media and marketing tools utilized by the seller's listing agent.

The companies that understand this rule of real estate use every tool imaginable to attract business, including "for sale" signs on properties, print advertising, marketing materials, mailers, and, yes, Internet sites. Real estate is still a local business because the real estate is local, and the company whose brand is recognizable and memorable will almost always have the first opportunity when a seller or a buyer is ready to talk about real estate needs.

We have been fortunate to build an internationally recognized franchise brand name that is another arrow in the quiver for local brokerages and agents to command the all-important control of the inventory and their marketplace.

THINK AHEAD AND BELIEVE IN YOURSELF

TERRY J. LUNDGREN

Terry J. Lundgren is chairman, president,
and CEO of Federated Department Stores, Inc.

The best real estate advice I ever received came from my father when I was twenty-six years old and considering the purchase of a home beyond my current means. My father told me to search the neighborhood in the particular area where I wanted to buy a home and to visit all six homes that were available for sale. Then he suggested that I rank them one through six and list the pros and cons of each property. My first choice was the perfect home and substantially more appealing than any others on the list. It was also substantially more expensive than the others on my list. I told my father that there was no sense considering it because I couldn't afford it. However, my father refused to talk about any of the other homes until we had considered all the possible ways of financing my first choice, which included taking out two mortgages with the bank and four separate trust deeds with balloon payments from the seller.

My father was encouraging me to bet on my future and focus not on my current payment capability but on what I would be able to pay over the next five years.

I bought that house and paid off the four trust deeds to the seller ahead of schedule, negotiating a reduced price from the original agreement in exchange for the early payment. When I sold the house years later, it was the best return on investment I ever experienced. This is not a strategy for everyone, but it was the right idea for me at that point in my life.

NEVER BE GREEDY

JOHN J. MACK
John J. Mack is chairman and CEO of Morgan Stanley.

Most of what I know about real estate I learned from my mother. She was a natural investor. She never had much money, but she had great instincts. In fact, if she had more money, she might have become a female Donald Trump.

I made my first property investment when I was in college. My mother and I borrowed money and bought residential lakefront lots in North Carolina, where we lived. It turned out to be a terrific investment—we earned a 40 percent return.

Over the years, I continued to follow my mother's lead on real estate. Probably the most valuable thing I learned along the way was: never be greedy. If you've done your homework and made a good deal, then take your profit and move on. If you start to be greedy, you eventually will get burned. In real estate, as in any business, your reputation is

153

the most important thing you own. To be successful over the long term, you need to do business in a way that earns you a reputation for quality, integrity, and honesty. It was good advice about real estate—and about life.

LISTEN TO YOURSELF

HARRY MACKLOWE

Harry Macklowe is founder, chairman, and CEO of Macklowe
Properties, Inc., an investment firm that focuses on upscale
commercial office and apartment properties in Manhattan
and owns the General Motors Building.

The best real estate advice I ever received was to listen to
yourself.

Real estate advice is usually self-generated and has
much to do with focusing on your vision and reaffirming
your objectives. Real estate is a chess game of extraordinary proportions. Encouragement should be most welcome, but it is rarely sought. Gaining support for your
convictions is a worthy challenge. An investor or a developer thrives on his or her private vision and the ability to
attain those goals. Along the way, courage and conviction
are the unwavering standards. Listen to yourself.

GO WITH YOUR GUT

BERNIE MARCUS

Bernie Marcus is cofounder of Home Depot and
chairman of the Marcus Foundation.

First, you carefully study the conclusions of the experts. Next, you thoroughly review the economic and demographic feasibility studies.

Then, you go with your gut. Throughout the years, many of the best decisions I've made were based on my common sense, good judgment, and the feeling in my gut that it was simply the right thing to do.

NEVER UNDERESTIMATE YOUR CLIENTS

ELIAS MASRI

Elias Masri is founder, chairman, and CEO of
Falcon Properties, Inc., a real estate management
corporation that manages 500,000 square feet of retail
and office space in the New York City area.

When I first arrived in New York from South America in 1977, speaking barely any English but with a very clear vision of what opportunities lay ahead in a depression-stricken New York City, I set out to buy several properties. I came with enough cash and a wealth of experience in real estate in a developing country that had always been ravaged by extremely fluctuating business cycles and unparalleled inflation rates, something that New York entrepreneurs were not accustomed to. As I began approaching sellers, their first reaction, after realizing I was an immigrant from a developing country, was dismissive and prejudiced.

At first, since I didn't fit into the stereotype of someone they believed was supposed to have enough money to invest in the commercial real estate market in the city, they barely even bothered to give any information on the buildings I was interested in buying. When they realized I had the money and the determination to buy, they would finally take me seriously and only then could we sit down and do business.

With that in mind, one of the most important pieces of advice I always give people who are in or who want to go into real estate is never to judge prospective clients by the way they look or act, or how well groomed or educated they seem. In all my fifty years in real estate, I have never underestimated any prospective client's ability and determination. As a matter of fact, many years ago back in my homeland, a man walked into my office dressed shabbily and carrying a supermarket bag in his hand. One of my employees quickly dismissed him and tried to turn him away. As I observed this scene, I approached the man and sat down with him. As it turned out, he was a senior executive of a very large local company who ended up buying an apartment that was even more expensive than the one he had originally inquired about!

I went on to buy twenty-five commercial buildings in west Midtown over the next twenty-five years. I bought buildings that the big New York real estate developers and entrepreneurs were not the least bit interested in. They were old, run-down buildings in blocks or areas of the city that were underdeveloped. With a combination of hard work, determination to get me through rough market fluctuations over the years, a vision, and a wealth of experience in real estate, I built my company solidly. The buildings I bought were renovated and restored from sweatshops to small offices and artists' studios.

From my own experience, the advice I would give is to have a vision of the place you want to develop, to find a niche of the market, with that perfect balance between taking some risk and betting on the future, yet always knowing your limitations and proceeding with enough caution to get you through rough economic periods. And above all, be humble.

CHOOSE EXCELLENT DESIGN— AND GOOD PLACEMENT

RICHARD MEIER

Richard Meier is a partner of Richard Meier & Partners Architects LLP. His projects include the Getty Center in Los Angeles and the Barcelona Museum of Contemporary Art. His many honors include the AIA Gold Medal from the American Institute of Architects and the Praemium Imperiale from the Japanese government.

I don't know about the best real estate advice I ever *received*, but the best real estate advice I could give would be to (1) hire an architect to create a high-quality environment, and (2) build it near the water. Do those two things and you will have made a wise investment.

One can't underestimate the correlation between the added value of good design and purchase price. Good design expresses the home buyers' desires before they themselves know what those desires are. People are willing to pay a premium to have those desires anticipated and realized. As an architect, I am always thrilled to work with a developer who understands what high-quality design means in terms of income over the life of a building, and who is willing to allow the architect to take the time to work through and develop a project's design to the highest possible standards.

MANAGE YOUR RISKS AND MAXIMIZE
YOUR RETURN ON INVESTMENT

DANIEL F. MIRANDA

Daniel F. Miranda is president of HSA Commercial Real Estate.

An older real estate developer and successful Chicago sports team owner and businessman told me that people often asked him which building among his dozens was the most attractive to him. Was it the one that won the architectural award? Was it the one that was designed by the most famous architect? Was it the one that was the largest of its type?

None of the above.

His consistent reply—"At the end of each year, my accountant tells me which of my buildings is the most beautiful."

Real estate is about accurately assessing and then jumping through the flaming hoops. Those who accurately measure the flame heat and hoop size can create value. Those who do not, fail and burn.

Although real estate's bottom line as a business is measured by risk-adjusted return or certainty of collecting and size of cash flow, getting to that point of cash flow or total return is the collective difficulty and the art of our business. All real estate decisions should be driven by the size of anticipated return on your investment adjusted for the risk. Accurately predicting or assessing the risk and potential return is both a mathematical calculation and an art form. If a company is able to accurately assess the many risks involved in real estate and then to reduce those risks by constantly monitoring, making appropriate decisions, and acting on those decisions, it will experience a better return on its investment.

I see it as a series of flaming hoops. The more difficulties there are, the greater the reward should be. Dealing with difficult land acquisition or unprecedented zoning challenges, developing complex financing, creating inventive marketing, turning around a failed project, negotiating with combative lenders, believing in success when most others are betting against you, and keeping up stamina to the payday—all are flaming hoops. Real estate developments with fewer hoops typically have a proportionately smaller yield. Those with more hoops should result in a greater yield.

The real estate organizations and the individuals with the greatest skill and stamina at appropriately assessing risk and then bringing a complete tool kit to the task of solving the risks are the ones who win.

MY FAVORITE "KIM-ISMS"

01

KIM MOGULL

Kim Mogull is president and CEO of Mogull Realty, Inc., a leader in representing marquee developers and retailers in New York, Florida, and select key markets throughout the United States.

I have never shied away from getting advice from the best and brightest—from clients, from friends, and from family. I've also had the privilege of observing brilliance in action. It is a pleasure to pass along some of the lessons I've learned along the way.

DO WHAT YOU LOVE AND YOU'LL NEVER WORK A DAY IN YOUR LIFE

People say I'm a workaholic. I say, "I'm just having fun." My mother, Martha Mogull, who remains my best friend and mentor, always encouraged me to pursue the kind of career that if I couldn't do for a living, I'd do for a hobby. The "hobby" of commercial real estate became my playground.

"No" Really Means "Convince Me"

I've always been a salesperson, and I've learned that people can be sold on any product if you give them the right reason to buy it. I first began honing my sales skills in elementary school while selling costume jewelry to teachers and classmates. In high school, I moved on to selling clocks out of the trunk of my car. And while attending Northwestern University, I became the number one door-to-door *Encyclopedia Britannica* salesperson in the Midwest. Although the product was different, the lesson remains the same: "No" really means "Convince me."

Move Your Inventory Fast

Even the best real estate appears stale when it sits too long because people just assume there is something wrong with it. In 2006 I brokered a joint venture for a hotel on the corner of Fifty-seventh Street and Sixth Avenue in New York City and simultaneously leased the vacant retail space to a celebrated restaurant group. The building owner had previously hired two major brokerage firms to fill the vacancy with no luck. The market's primary objection was that Fifty-seventh Street and Sixth Avenue was "an unlucky, dead corner." Of course it was dead—it had been vacant for years! The vacancy, combined with the momentum of other false objections, caused the market to turn a blind eye to the highly trafficked site near Carnegie Hall and Central Park.

Once hired, I immediately spruced up the building, wrapping it with a huge purple ribbon and bow along with a sign that read, "Our gift to you—a brand new restaurant for no key money." Among those I contacted was the owner of The James Hotel Group, one of the hottest new boutique hotels expanding across the country. We soon formed a joint venture to convert the site to The James' flag and leased the retail space to a major restaurateur. The previously "dead" corner will emerge as one of New York City's most vibrant.

Create Excitement and a Sense of Urgency About Your Product

In one of Donald's previous books, *TRUMP: The Way to the Top*, Barbara Corcoran offered great advice when she said, "When there are ten buyers and three puppies, every dog is the pick of the litter." Well said, Barbara. My favorite way of showing space is through back-to-back showings with prospects coming in one after the other. This not only maximizes your time, it creates a sense of urgency and inflated demand.

Make It Memorable; Make It Fun; Make It Productive

When I sold encyclopedias door-to-door, I used to take a wrapped-up gift—usually a little dictionary. People were so curious to unwrap the gift that they would let me in the door. A $3 pocket dictionary would wind up costing them a minimum of $1,099—the price of our least expensive set of encyclopedias. Nothing has changed. When I visit my real estate clients, I often come armed with something unexpected that the person will appreciate. It's usually something that personally touches the client or sparks their imagination. But I also always come prepared to back up the incidentals with something of value—information—something my client would want to know but didn't before I arrived. This is a way of adding value while keeping a smile on their face.

NEVER LOSE SIGHT OF THE HUMAN SIDE OF A DEAL

Selling real estate is not just placing a piece of property with a buyer or tenant; it is bringing two people together. Even in a corporate transaction, the decision to make or break a deal is made by people. No matter how tight your schedule or your clients' time, do your best to have face-to-face meetings. It is much easier to kill a "faceless deal." And above all, act honorably. That is what people remember.

MY MOTHER ALWAYS SAID, "FROM LITTLE ACORNS BIG TREES GROW"

Many people have asked me, "How did you get Donald Trump's business?" I got it through preparation, passion, and persistence—plus seventeen years of practicing commercial real estate 24/7 and loving it. When Mr. Trump's office first called to request a meeting with me, I was president of a small real estate company. I went to my first meeting with Donald knowing everything I could about his retail portfolio. I also told him where I thought I could add value. After one hour of classic Donald Trump interrogation (causing sweating, nausea, and slight hyperventilation), I was hired—but only for one store. I had one chance to prove myself and was assured that if I did, more business would follow. Once hired, I immediately began implementing my plan and proving myself one store at a time.

Don't Be Afraid to Trust Your Instincts or Spend Money to Make Money

My first assignment from Donald was to lease a corner restaurant at Trump Plaza. But when I walked through the space for the first time, my radar went off because a restaurant didn't belong there. Furthermore, the store seemed bigger than what I had been told. I was nervous about giving Donald advice because he barely knew me, and my competitor had been marketing the vacant restaurant "as-is" at the smaller square footage. I advised Donald to hire an architect to remeasure the space and a contractor to gut it. If I was wrong, he would never hire me again. I stuck to my instincts, and they were right. The space was larger than I had been told. We doubled our rent and blew through previous income projections.

ABOVE ALL, BE PASSIONATE; PASSION IS CONTAGIOUS

The day I was hired, Donald not only gave me a great opportunity but also the best business advice I've ever received. As I was leaving his office, he said, "Kim, you're one of the greatest salespeople I've ever met. Start your own company. Brand yourself. Make it easy for people to find you." The next day I formed Mogull Realty with Donald as my first client. I've never looked back.

It took years to win his trust—years of working hard and smart. The bottom line is the bottom line, and clients like Donald reward results. Years and many transactions later, Mogull Realty has become the exclusive broker for the bulk of the Trump Organization's retail portfolio.

GO WHERE YOU'RE NEEDED

BRUCE E. MOSLER

Bruce E. Mosler is president and CEO of Cushman & Wakefield, the global real estate services firm.

Back in 1996 when I was president of the eastern region of the Galbraith Company, my firm was sold, and I was looking for alternatives in the marketplace. I had boiled it down to two firms: one was Cushman & Wakefield, and the other was a competing firm. Donald Trump told me, "I think you need to go to Cushman & Wakefield." The suggestion was that you should go where you are needed, not where you are wanted.

The fundamental difference between the two is very simple: lots of companies want to hire key people for their organization for many different reasons—some because it will keep those people out of another organization, others because those people will add temporary value. But in the long run, if you go where you're needed, you contribute the most sustainable value. That was a very good piece of advice from him, and at the time I was coming to Cushman & Wakefield only as a broker. As it turns out, the need was such that I eventually became CEO. You can't get better advice than that.

LEAD BY EXAMPLE

One of my mentors was Alvin Dorman, a very successful developer who was and is the developer for Bacara, which is a destination resort in Santa Barbara, California. He is also a very successful residential and commercial developer around the country. Alvin taught me two things. One was to lead by example. On a most fundamental level, that means when you lead people, you have to have walked in their shoes. In my case, I'm leading a global brokerage company of more than eleven thousand people. I am a broker. I have been in the field. I have represented tenants. I know the ups and downs. I know the resourcing necessary. But certainly the advice in terms of walking the walk and having experienced the experience is absolutely necessary to get the collective buy-in of the people you are leading. That has always been something I've taken with me.

FOCUS ON ONE AREA

The other essential thing that Alvin taught me was to become an expert in your industry. In my arena of commercial real estate, you can be a generalist, but to reach the top, you have to focus on one area of the business. Our business is broad—it's investment sales; it's appraisal; it's commercial leasing; it's facilities management and asset management. I chose tenant representation as the one component part of the field on which to focus.

THINK BRANDING

The final piece is the best advice that I ever got from my father, and it's a big cliché, but it's factual. My father was the chairman of Mosler Safe, which was a very well-known business. He always felt that the brand means everything; everything you do has to enhance the brand, and everything you do will affect the brand. How you conduct yourself, what you are, and who you are—all are related directly to the brand of the business.

THINK LOCATION—AND HONESTY

DAVID MOSSLER

David Mossler is chairman of Mossler & Doe, which represents and sells estates, historic and architectural residential properties primarily in Southern California.

When you are purchasing real estate, the three most important rules remain: location, location, location.

When you are selling real estate, the three most important rules are: disclose, disclose, disclose. Honesty prevails.

BUY—AND WAIT

TERRI MURPHY

Terri Murphy is a professional speaker, the CIO of U.S.
Learning in Memphis, and a writer for *Broker Agent News*,
Mortgage Originator Magazine, *Realty Times*, and
Memphis Woman magazines.

The great Cavett Robert, founder of the National Speakers Association and longtime entrepreneur, made a statement that is one of my personal favorites: "Don't wait to buy real estate—buy real estate and wait." This solid advice has worked for me and many of my clients for years.

With the exception of encountering a man-made disaster such as Chernobyl that impacts the real estate market, real estate generally increases in value. Some areas such as California may increase more quickly than others such as Dubuque, Iowa, but for the most part, real estate increases in value.

Most regular people (sorry, Donald, not you!) invest in

their own residences but fail to leverage their financial well-being through additional real estate investments.

There are three steps I recommend to support Cavett's advice to buy real estate and wait:

Step 1: Start with a plan. Begin with a plan built on whether your strategy is to invest in a property for the long term or the short term. You can choose to hold a property for the long run or to hold it for a short time and flip the property for short-term profit.

If you plan to *hold* a property for several years, your strategy would expect annual appreciation and consistent rental income to pay off the mortgage debt and give you an income. However, if you plan to hold a property for the long term, you will need to consider hiring a professional property management company; setting aside funds for repairs, replacements, and upkeep; reserving funds to cover gaps in rental income in case of vacancies; and taking into account the effect of neighborhood values in the long term. If a property is in an area with good tenant traffic—close to town and schools, and within walking distance to transportation—you are more likely to ensure incremental increase of rental income.

If you plan to hold a property for several years, you should study the benefits of a mortgage with a shorter amortization schedule so that you can pay it off in a shorter, more specific period of time. If you can afford a mortgage with a ten- to twenty-year amortization, it can create positive cash flow more quickly than a traditional thirty-year loan. Your strategy may be to acquire a number of properties using other property equity as leverage to secure additional investment funds. A long-term hold plan can provide financial freedom. A plan to hold a property for a short term (flipping) can be a terrific way to generate cash, but a more solid strategy is to secure income properties in a good area with consistent rental income, and then let the real estate work for you. Before you know it, ten years will pass, and with smart investment practices, you will enjoy solid appreciation on properties that someone else paid for every month, offering you the gift of letting real estate and your money work for you.

Beginning real estate investors usually purchase a home for themselves and their families. This purchase is a step to investment and can be used to help acquire additional real estate. However, most people give more thought to buying holiday gifts than to thinking through a real estate purchase.

Exercise a little due diligence, and determine your overall financial objective. Are you planning to live in this real estate, and, if so, how long? The answer to this question will help define the best strategy. Consider factors such as the type of financing, the local market history, local zoning, new construction starts, and so forth. Think through such factors and do your homework. If you are single, you want to build a real estate portfolio, and you are starting modestly with a place to live. Use that time to learn about the duties and obligations of property ownership, to keep good credit, and to initiate and build relationships that will facilitate future investments.

Step 2: Build a team of experts. It has never been easier to learn about how to invest in real estate while you have a "day job." The Internet, books, real estate seminars, and other opportunities can meet your needs. The best advice is to build your *team* of experts because real estate is a many-faceted adventure. You can't know it all! Trying to do it all on your own can be a tough lesson on the ego and the wallet when investing without the proper due diligence.

Interview and prospect for team members as you would for business partners. Interview real estate agents, developers, appraisers, loan originators, bankers, accountants, and attorneys specializing in real estate before you begin prospecting for properties. Select the experts that suit your style. Every area has its own nuances that affect the value of the local real estate. These nuances may be generally known by locals and not listed in public records or in real estate investment books. Having a team in whom you have confidence will make prospecting and purchasing much smoother.

When I moved to Memphis from Chicago, I managed

to find a great place in a gated community where properties were not available very often. The property was being sold by the owner, but after we agreed on the purchase price, the property failed to appraise for as much as I had offered. That was good for me, but bad for her because the value of this property has almost doubled in less than twenty-four months. However, other properties in surrounding areas have barely increased by 2 to 3 percent a year. The message is: study, ask questions, and study some more before making an investment. The old adage "location, location, location" is still on target!

Step 3: Work your plan. Use your investment guidelines to build your portfolio, assemble the best team to help you make the best decisions, and block time on a regular basis to continue to study the market. Many new investors underestimate the importance of the regular time and attention required to invest successfully in real estate. Many investors with whom I've consulted purchase property that is managed by a property management company and then fail to check annually on property values, to study the maintenance required, to project long-term functional obsolescence, and to evaluate competition from new and proposed construction in the area. And they wonder if they are making any money. This is *not* a good plan!

There is one thing you can be sure of: real estate changes every day. It does not change as fast as the stock market, but something impacts real estate daily: company layoffs, new company start-ups, public transportation, new taxes, new schools, new shopping centers, and renovations of downtown areas.

The best real estate advice I ever received was to buy real estate and wait. In ten years, acquiring only one property per year, even a modest investment will allow you to earn money while you sleep and often at a much faster rate than you could make working really hard! When you pay close attention, your investment labor will pay you. And as Cavett says, enjoy earning while you wait. Good luck!

ASSESS YOUR RISKS

85

JOSHUA L. MUSS

Joshua L. Muss is president of Muss Development Company, one of the largest ongoing development companies in New York City.

For many years, development in New York City was dominated by real estate families; longevity was necessary to accumulate experience and capital, and to see through interest rate cycles, marketplace slumps, and entitlement periods that could last decades . . . and more.

My grandfather Isaac Muss came to America in 1906. He began to build extensively in Brooklyn until the Great Depression took its toll on his success. My father, Hyman, one of eleven siblings, continued in the family trade after World War II. Funding was limited; projects were modest. Stick-built residential sales fueled commercial ventures, one project at a time.

Upon my graduation from law school, after a five-year apprenticeship of silent adulation and obeisance during which I knew that all he did was right, there followed a five-year period when—by my estimation—everything Hyman Muss did was wrong! We built the wrong things in the wrong places. No sex appeal. Not big enough. What we needed was a money partner to put us into the "big time." My father's response: "If a project is good, you don't need a partner. If a project is bad, you don't want a partner."

Many decades later, and many projects wiser, I reflect on those words that have permeated my thinking. As a consequence of following his advice (he *was* the boss), I sought out larger projects that were "without risk." The process was simple: find inexpensive land, obtain zoning changes and environmental clearance, line up users, finish up with the construction, and reap the profits. As long as it took. Simple. Sometimes.

Life, however, in the last decade of the twentieth century and the early 2000s has become a bit more complex. No more "conventional" financing. The development families are being supplemented, if not replaced, by REITs (real estate investment trusts), opportunity funds, and large public corporations; patient money has given way to calculated double-digit IRRs (internal rate of returns); projects are measured by the hundreds of millions of dollars. Daily, new entrepreneurs with limited experience and with even less capital are leveraging mega developments with mega equity partners.

And yet I continue to heed my father's advice . . . with

some modification: I assess every project as if the risk is to be mine to fund and to complete. When I am satisfied that a project is good and can proceed without a partner, I invite participation. In today's world of real estate development, you "need" and you "want" partners. Good partnerships will help Muss Development reach for another one hundred years.

SEEK OUT GOOD ARCHITECTURE

ENRIQUE NORTEN

Enrique Norten founded TEN Arquitectos in Mexico City in
1986 and later opened a second office in New York. He currently
holds the Miller Chair at the University of Pennsylvania and
is Eero Saarinen Visiting Professor of Architectural Design
at the Yale School of Architecture.

We all hear that the best advice is to select the best site,
and it's true that location is a very important part. But
I think that good architecture and good design will always
sell better. I truly believe that, especially in sophisticated
markets like New York City and other global cities, good
architecture always has a premium in the market. Better
architecture and better design go faster and sell higher than
just plain vanilla. Good architecture and a good location
will be even better.

REMEMBER THAT REAL ESTATE IS A CYCLICAL BUSINESS

ELAN PADEH

Elan Padeh is president and CEO of The Developers Group and has served as principal, landlord, developer, and consultant in the residential and commercial markets.

The formula for everyone who is truly successful in real estate is simple, but carrying out that formula is anything but easy. The formula? Find out everything you can about the product, the neighborhood, and the market. Define your clients and figure out what their hot buttons are. Determine what parts of the financial, construction, and development industries can work to the advantage of your clients, whether they are buyers, investors, or developers. Never forget that experience can't be overestimated, and never, never get into the game for a quick buck.

It is crucial to remember that real estate is a cyclical business. People who talk about "bubbles" simply haven't spent enough time in the business to understand completely how it works. Even at its peak, real estate is a viable investment for *someone*, and the wise investor or developer knows enough about the cycles to know when the time is right for his or her individual situation. In 2006, for example, the prices were too high for many potential landlords. That doesn't mean, though, that no one was able or willing to buy. Instead, it means that almost everyone in that market was representing a fund or an individual who could wait three decades to realize the gain on the investment or was involved in a 1031 Exchange.

Moreover, I believe strongly that wise investors buy and hold. While flipping gets a lot of media attention in a market such as we've had in recent years and may result in a gain, the significant returns will go to those who buy, hold, and rent, and then choose their time to sell.

For developers, this is a fascinating time to be in this business, especially in New York. People are living longer, and more and more of them are moving to the New York area. People with vision can redefine boundaries in ways that can be remunerative. An area that may have been considered to be irretrievably depressed, such as Bedford Stuyvesant, today beckons for new development by those who can see the potential and know how to go after it. I'm sure there are similar areas in other large metropolitan areas throughout the United States.

Another demographic change of which my partners

and I have taken advantage is that five to ten years ago, some informed parents recognized that it would be a great investment to buy a condo for their twenty-something children, who would then pay rent to defray carrying costs. The parents would reap the rewards of escalating prices, but their offspring—young, excited, and opinionated—chose which apartments to live in. What's more, those same young people would most probably be making a buying choice within a decade, and so pleasing them once could mean selling them twice. Because their tastes are different, knowing how to configure space and then design it so that it appeals to them is a key to real success.

When these young people do get ready to buy, their financial position can make it a challenge for them to buy what they really want. My partners and I have found that formerly depressed areas can hold great potential. For instance, state and federal requirements allow bankers to finance properties in a depressed area at rates one to two points below the current market rate. But what constitutes a "depressed area" can change more rapidly in reality than the U.S. Census Bureau assessment of a "depressed area" changes. So, if an area is up and coming, savvy bankers can make loans at very appealing rates, garner hip, young customers, and create a win-win situation.

A little creative thought can reap huge rewards for developers. Young clients want one to two bedrooms, but they may not be very selective about the precise configuration. A developer can—and should—make that work to his advantage. For example, if the configuration of a two-bedroom condo is the traditional "railroad" style, corridor space consumes valuable square feet. If, instead, a two-bedroom condo is what we refer to as a "split," the space is maximized. The total square footage in a railroad-style condo might be 1,125, compared to 1,050 square feet in a split condo with the same size rooms. If a building has a total of 100 apartments and 50 of those are splits, the developer has saved 3,750 square feet of build-out costs, which can be more than $2 million depending on build-out costs. Wisdom calls for simultaneously configuring to suit the client and maximize efficiency. The consulting that my partners and I do is all about that.

Really successful people in real estate, no matter what part they play, do two things: work hard, and love their work. Starting a business is a scary proposition, but with the right kind of enthusiasm and plain old hard work, the results are more than you dream they could be. I love my work, and I choose to work only with other people who do too. Yes, we like the money we make, but money is more a by-product than a goal. Real estate is a life-consuming enterprise that pays back handsomely for every minute you spend.

IN THE FUTURE, EVERYTHING WILL BE VERY SMALL AND VERY FAST!

JOHN M. PECKHAM III

John M. "Jack" Peckham is executive director of the 10,000-member Real Estate CyberSpace Society (REcyber.com).

C ome see this!"

In 1994 a man at a tech trade show said it to anyone who would listen: "Come see this!" He was fiddling with a brand-new computer program called Mosaic that zipped him around the Internet by simply clicking on little images. When he stepped aside, I grabbed the mouse, and with two clicks I was catapulted across the Internet to information I needed from a library in Pretoria, South Africa. Knowing how I had spent more than a year trying to navigate the Internet by typing in long, complicated commands, I whistled softly and said to him, "This is going to change my real estate industry in ways we can't even imagine today!"

Making the Most of Information

Encouraging me to use the growing power and ease of the Internet to gather, understand, and disseminate information is the best real estate advice I received. Way back in 1963, I founded Data Realty Corp., a real estate brokerage firm that racked up hundreds of millions of dollars in real estate investment property sales. Our secret was that we used an old IBM sorter and keypunch to allow us to match real estate investors with property that fit their criteria. The computing power of that rig was almost nothing compared with what is available today, but the press and the industry thought we were miracle workers because of the speed with which we could match up information.

Until 1996 everyone involved in real estate quoted the age-old mantra—"It's location, location, location!" In that one moment two years earlier on the trade show floor, I intuitively knew that the winners of the real estate war, although not ignoring the old location, location, location rule, would eventually pick up the mantra of the cyber-space age—"It's information, information, information." On this premise, in 1996, we founded www.REcyber.com, the Real Estate CyberSpace Society, which has grown to more than 10,000 members in 120 chapters.

For those in the real estate business, the information and the speed with which one can disseminate and obtain the information are powerful tools. Shortly after finding eight buyers in three hours for a $2.6 million Walgreens investment property using the Internet, I set out to develop Internet information broadcasting tools at the Society.

I still hear the echoes of "Come see this!" urging me to explore the tools of the Internet. For example, the Society quickly provided its members with powerful deal-making tools such as the E-Mail Broadcast Wizard. Using this tool, commercial real estate broker and investor members can instantly send one message that broadcasts their investment properties for sale, or send their investment needs to a list of more than 55,000 recipients who have requested specific positioning in 55 different broadcast lists, all without spamming.

SAVING TIME AND MONEY

The success of this tool has demonstrated the power of the Internet to get information into the appropriate hands immediately. Internet marketing gurus describe this instant marketing as "push marketing" because it puts information right in the recipient's face without the need for the recipient to go anyplace or do anything other than open his e-mail. And the other advantage of this form of marketing is that it is free!

When I compared this method of instantly disseminating information, for example, to 10,000 logical recipients on a real estate investment for sale with the traditional method of printing brochures, stuffing them into envelopes, addressing the envelopes, sticking stamps on them, and lugging the pile to the post office, I could easily see the many benefits of electronic instant communication. The advantage of speed, bullet targeting, and "in your face" delivery is surpassed only by the cost advantage. Using traditional methods, the cost of reaching 10,000 potential buyers might be $10,000. Using instant communication methods such as the Real Estate CyberSpace Society's E-Mail Broadcast Wizard, the cost for each mailing is essentially zero!

The Real Buyer Direct program is another example of a powerful and highly useful information resource. It allows real estate investors and brokers to instantly target the appropriate buyers for a particular property—or to find the most logical sellers for a particular type of property they are looking for. The Society maintains the database and gives members the ability to select the appropriate list of buyers or potential sellers from the database of more than 8,000 and immediately send one e-mail message to the selected list—all in less than two minutes. The power of the Internet to gather and disseminate information now gives both smaller investors and brokers equal access to information that was once available only to firms with deep pockets.

In the very near future we will witness the impact of audio and video information feeds through RSS (Really Simple Syndication), which allows podcasting as a way to put even more information instantly in the recipient's face. Combine this with the integration of reception and delivery of multiple information tools into what are now quite simple cell phones. We will witness the continuing integration of today's cell phones, paging systems, PDAs, mapping devices, people trackers, personal security systems, MP3 players, RSS systems, television receivers, and data projectors that project images, slide shows, or videos onto a holographic screen in the air in front of us accompanied by surround-sound. And other devices will be created with functions we can hardly envision today.

INCREASING SPEED AND DECREASING SIZE

Several years ago, I was preparing to deliver the keynote address to five hundred members of the CCIM Institute at their annual educational conference in Toronto. That evening many CCIM members were accompanied by their families, including about twenty children. Because magic has been my hobby for several decades, I often use a couple of "miracles" as part of my talks. That night I asked the event organizers to create a small open space in front of the riser where I was to deliver my talk and to assemble the children (ranging in age from three to thirteen) there, seated on the floor.

With the five hundred attendees hushed after I was introduced, I asked them to sit back and watch for a couple of minutes before my talk because I wanted to do a couple of tricks for the children. In the course of my mini magic show, I asked the children how many thought they would go into the real estate business like their mom or dad. Three of nineteen children raised their hands (the twentieth was asleep).

Spotting a spare chair near me on the stage, I took a huge chance and, with no script or plan, invited an eleven-year-old girl who had indicated that she might get into real estate onto the stage with me. The five hundred real estate pros watched.

I shared the microphone with her as we chatted briefly, and her sincerity impressed me. Then I took the biggest risk of my speaking experience. I asked her what she thought the real estate business would be like at the time she would be entering it in ten or fifteen years. I held my breath, knowing that if she wanted, she could give me a blank "Are you crazy?" look or just say, "I have no idea," leaving the whole impromptu exercise flat as a pancake!

But she didn't. She looked at me with all the sincerity an eleven-year-old can muster, without missing a beat, and very matter-of-factly said, "Everything will be very small and very fast!"

In those simple words she described the future better than all of the touted prognosticators rolled into one. I still get chills when I think about her description of the future for real estate. Think about it every once in a while, and I'll bet you will too.

The tools we have today enable both real estate investors and brokers in ways I couldn't have imagined when that stranger said, "Come see this!" on that tech trade show floor in 1994.

Now I give this advice: "Come see this!" The changes we have seen since 1994 will pale into insignificance when we see how rapidly change will affect our real estate industry in the next five years. We will gather, organize, arrange, and present information in ways that will help perfect the accuracy of our real estate decision-making process. And everything will be very small and very fast!

KNOWLEDGE, ENTHUSIASM, INTEGRITY, AND HARD WORK

SUSAN PENZNER

Susan Penzner is president of Susan Penzner Real Estate,
and she has been active in SoHo, Tribeca, and Chelsea
real estate since 1978. She is a member of the
Real Estate Board of New York.

To be successful in real estate, one needs three essential elements: knowledge, enthusiasm, and integrity.

1. *Knowledge.* The accepted wisdom is that until you know the product, whether it is residential or commercial, and the market in which it is being sold, you cannot begin to serve your clients adequately. What isn't always recognized is that the "product" is as much the neighborhood as the individual living or working space. In essence, you are selling comfort. Knowing the best dry cleaner, the most creative florist, the most efficient copy center, and the most reliable caterer is as important as determining the construction quality, the access to public transportation, or

the spatial configuration. Many individuals begin their real estate career, especially on the residential side, by concentrating on the area where they live. That is smart for the very reason that their knowledge is then based on personal experience, which is far more reliable than the most sophisticated research.

I am reminded of an experience some years ago when keeping a valid real estate license in the city of New York required taking refresher courses. Donald Trump was one of the featured speakers for a course I took. Having just finished the Hyatt Hotel next to Grand Central Station, he brought with him the full array of business associates who worked with him on the project—architect, engineer, and so on. The presentation was fascinating, and I came away with the firm realization that underlying his success was the ability to gather the best information from the brightest people.

2. *Enthusiasm.* Before I became involved in real estate, I was in the fashion and art worlds. I was attracted to real estate in part because of my love for design and architecture. Although I opened my office on the Upper East Side of New York where I lived, I knew a great deal about SoHo as well because of my affiliation with *Art Forum* magazine. Artists' lofts are now a part of what SoHo is all about, but I was selling lofts in the early days when they were a way to bridge the gap between the income of young—and not so

young—artists and their aesthetic tastes. Selling lofts was the result of my innate enthusiasm for interesting architecture, combined with my delight in dealing with very interesting people. It is incredibly important to love what you sell and enjoy being with the people to whom you sell it.

This is true of commercial as well as residential sales. Successfully working with a retail space is every bit as much a matter of knowing it is a "fit" for your client as it is negotiating a favorable rate. I must like the product to sell it. Because that is true, I have been able to build a strong referral business.

The trend today takes this formula one remarkable step further. What is being sold—certainly in New York, and I assume in other cities as well—is a lifestyle, a sense of design. Fashion designers are asked to create lobbies. Famed architects are part and parcel of redevelopment. The Gramercy Park Project in New York is an elegant and most exciting example.

3. *Integrity.* *Integrity* is an overused term, but that doesn't make it any less important. The problem, unfortunately, is that many associate integrity only with honesty. Dealing forthrightly and ethically is not only right, but crucial. To me, though, integrity is much more. For example, I have a number of clients who are quite well known in theater, motion pictures, and fashion design. I have never felt comfortable publicizing my work with them because their

privacy is far more important than the value of having my name associated with theirs. Yes, there have been times when a reporter has connected my name with one of these people, but it has not been and will never be because I encourage it.

Moreover, when I hire people to work with me, I look for the kind of person who will bring that same attitude to the relationship. My associates must work with clients as I would, so that clients are just as comfortable with them. Certainly I want my associates to bring their own style and creativity to what they do, but the work and how we do it are about designing a lively, interesting, and lasting relationship with every client.

While it takes hard work, a willingness and the financial ability to wait for the business to build, especially on the commercial side, and unending equanimity, real estate is a rewarding career.

BE OBJECTIVE; BE REALISTIC; ALWAYS LEAVE SOMETHING ON THE TABLE

JORGE PEREZ

Jorge Perez is founder, chairman, and CEO of The Related Group of Florida, the nation's leading builder of luxury condominiums and the largest Hispanic-owned business in the United States.

Never get "emotionally married" to your real estate deal. Maintain your objectivity, do all the analysis, and if it does not generate the economic returns you require, pass on it. Never look back.

Not just in real estate, but in life in general, a deal is never as good as it seems or as bad as it seems. Keep your expectations in line with reality.

Always leave something on the table.

STOP TALKING AND GET IT DONE!

DAVID PICERNE
David Picerne is CEO of Picerne Real Estate Group,
a provider of high-quality housing in markets throughout
the United States and Puerto Rico.

Everyone talks about vision. For me, it's implementation. Assemble a team of bright, hardworking people, and "Get 'er done!"

DON'T LET THE MARKET CONTROL YOU

ROBIN E. PRESCOD

Robin E. Prescod is managing partner of Harlem Homes, Inc.

The best real estate advice I ever received came from my own experience: don't allow the market to control your deal; flip the scenario to have your deal create the market.

I have a client with a unique piece of property in Harlem: a twenty-foot-wide brownstone, four stories with high ceilings, ten rooms, a formal dining room, and six fireplaces. Unlike most Harlem brownstones that have only north and south exposures, this one is on a courtyard so it actually has three exposures and a private driveway that can park three cars. It is on Strivers' Row, a name that dates back to the first Harlem Renaissance in the 1920s when wealthy doctors, lawyers, and musicians lived there.

My client noticed a lot of people coming into Harlem, buying properties, doing some renovation, and then flipping them for $2 million. But those houses did not have the ambience and distinction of this historic landmarked home. So I decided to market it to celebrities, who have that kind of desire and who would need that type of exclusive living and privacy—they could pull their limousine into a private driveway and slip into their back door. I marketed it in *Billboard* and in high-end real estate periodicals to attract music industry stars or sports stars.

It's on the market at $2.7 million, and we'll sell it because Harlem continues to be the uptown destination of choice.

LEARN TO RECOGNIZE VALUE

BILL RANCIC

Bill Rancic was the first winner of Donald Trump's reality television show *The Apprentice*. He cofounded Cigars Around the World and is the author of *You're Hired: How to Succeed in Business and Life from the Winner of The Apprentice*.

I've spent the past two years working with Mr. Trump, being his apprentice. And I've been very fortunate because he's taken me under his wing and he's introduced me to his strategies and his ways of working in real estate.

One of the projects I've been working on is the Trump International Hotel and Tower in Chicago. One thing about Donald Trump is he's able to recognize value and he's able to create value. I think that's probably the key to being successful in real estate. The prime example is the project here in Chicago. He was able to look at the site, which he was able to buy at a very good price, and saw an eight-story building where he could create some value. Now he's putting up a ninety-two-story building on that plot of land.

Not only is Donald Trump able to create value, but he is also able to think big. A lot of people fall short because they don't think big enough. For Donald Trump, obviously, that's never been a problem. He's able to do that. There are always going to be people who are doubting and who say it can't be done, but he's a guy who doesn't give up.

BUY LAND AND BANK IT, BUT DO
YOUR HOMEWORK FIRST

HENRY ROBBINS

Henry Robbins is a partner at Yale Robbins, Inc.,
a real estate publisher.

We got into this game thirty years ago when my brother, Yale, decided to develop a real estate consulting business. Having been a successful real estate broker, Yale realized he did not particularly like the pace of constantly playing in extra innings. He would receive assignments from builders who needed feasibility studies for sites. We then changed our approach so that rather than being paid a one-time fee to analyze one situation, we created a service that provided in-depth information that was usable by lots of people. We charge a smaller fee per customer but have many more customers. We eventually covered commercial real estate as well as residential and developed new delivery mechanisms—first print and then electronic.

In 1976 our company was a pioneer by developing a

subscription service that provided analysis of residential real estate on a dollars-per-square-foot basis as opposed to dollars-per-room. Today, all residential real estate is evaluated by a dollars-per-square-foot basis. Our philosophy was straightforward: make available at a reasonable cost a lot of information at once. That's how we became a bricks-and-clicks firm.

I have seen lots of developers come and go, and I've noticed that there are two types of people who make it big in the real estate game: those who are good, and those who are lucky. Sometimes you have to be both. But the really heavy hitters have a sort of sixth sense. They can see the potential of a property way before anyone else does. Beauty is in the eye of the beholder, and real estate is too. Time after time you hear, "He's nuts. How could he pay that much for that property? He's going to lose his shirt." Five years later the developer who paid "too much" banks the money—a lot of it.

You cannot really learn or buy that kind of vision any more than you can buy athletic prowess. We can't all be Michael Jordan or Donald Trump. When you've got it, you've got it, and you're ahead of the game from the beginning.

On the other hand, it is true that anyone who bought property ten years ago in New York City pretty much couldn't make a mistake. And so my advice is to buy land

and bank it. Purchase property and just sit back for five years or so. Time and again I've watched an owner make even more than the developer—and with fewer headaches or risks.

Of course, real estate is a local market. What plays on Broadway won't play in West Virginia. What you learn from one phone call from a national office somewhere won't work everywhere. You need foot soldiers, good ones, who know what's going on in the areas you're targeting. We publish information about real estate in ten states, and to different mind-sets and attitudes.

One thing that is pretty universal, though, is that the commercial market drives the residential market. A healthy commercial market means more jobs, and those people can then buy housing. But different forces drive the market at different times in different places. Staying on top of the information game feeds that vision I discussed earlier. Even the people we describe as lucky won't get there without doing their homework.

EIGHT RULES OF REAL ESTATE SUCCESS

PHIL RUFFIN

Phil Ruffin is CEO and owner of Ruffin Companies,
which includes varied real estate, lodging, manufacturing,
energy, and retail enterprises.

1. Once a seller has signed a contract, even with contingencies, the person has mentally sold the property. Once the contract is signed, there are always ways to renegotiate the deal. List your litany of problems—environment, roof issues, heating and air, and so forth. Come back with a new, lower price *as is*. You can always go back to your original offer.

2. Go where the money is; play only in those markets.

3. Sell only if you need the money. The property you are selling is worth more than the money.

4. When negotiating, remember the pause. Always hesitate on a key point. The other side will hate the silence and will think you are balking. Wait for the other person to speak and cave in.

5. Don't buy property just because it is cheap. It is better to play at the top end of the market (premium locations). Cheaper properties will not make the kind of money you seek. Premium properties even at current market rates will seem cheap in a couple of years.

6. Sellers will often carry some paper (it is worth a try).

7. Make sure you have a property you want to buy (and the price) before you do a 1031 Exchange. If not, you will probably end up with something undesirable.

8. Partner with Trump if you can. The name sells like mad.

SOLID SALESMANSHIP, AN ENTREPRENEURIAL SPIRIT, AND YEARS OF EXPERIENCE

PETER SABESAN

Peter Sabesan is CEO of The Hunter Realty Organization, LLC.

Solid salesmanship, an entrepreneurial spirit, and years of experience are the three parts of the pie when it comes to real estate success as I see it.

Real estate is all about salesmanship, and, although a big part of salesmanship is personality, it also involves developing some important skills. For instance, my dad taught me long ago that it is crucial to know when to stop talking and listen to someone. The twenty or so salespeople who work for us now hear this from me over and over.

Every owner is different; every tenant is different. You can't persuade someone who is convinced he only wants to be on the West Side of Manhattan to look on the East Side if you don't know why he feels that way. What's more important, you can lose the deal by talking about great properties on the East Side because you haven't stopped to listen to find out he's got his eyes to the West.

Another crucial element is entrepreneurial spirit. My partner and I started our company to simply create an income stream while we decided which firm we would go with next. We already had almost two decades of experience, and we both knew there is nothing harder to sell than commercial real estate. This is a feast-or-famine business. The big, good firms pretty much have the large metropolitan markets sewn up. That was nine years ago, though, and we've managed to thrive as a much smaller enterprise focused exclusively on New York.

However, in no way would I discredit any of the major firms. In fact, if a person just entering the business asked me how to proceed, I'd say that starting out on your own is foolish. Go learn from the pros. But when you are in the business, trade on what you bring to the table that is different.

When we negotiate, for example, we make it clear that every transaction our clients have with us will include a partner. The people who show up for the first meeting are the same for the fifth. In large firms, that's not the procedure, and it's what makes us different.

Just recently, we had a customer who had had someone tell him that with the market strengthening he should raise his rents beyond what he'd agreed to. He called, and we met with him. We didn't send a salesman, though we've got great salesmen who are anything but shabby at negotiating. We reinforced the fact that we had the experience he could depend on, and he agreed to stand by his earlier decision.

NEVER LOSE PATIENCE

HENRY SAVAGE

Henry Savage is founder and president of PMC Mortgage Corporation, a licensed residential mortgage lender and broker. He writes columns for Realtytimes.com and *Washington Times* Friday Home Guide.

Over time, real estate has proven to be a good investment. But it's a game of patience. Natural appreciation isn't guaranteed, especially over the short term. Creating value through improvements and/or renovation can be delayed in the event of a downturn.

There is something very true in the saying "The bigger the boom, the bigger the bust." This is something to remember for those who are jumping on the real estate bandwagon, expecting to double their money in twelve months. Keep your overhead under control. Make sure you have staying power. Cycles happen.

KEEP AN UPBEAT ATTITUDE

RONDA SAVOY

Ronda Savoy is owner of Ronda Savoy Realty, Inc., a real estate firm whose specialty is Brownstone Brooklyn. She is a member of the Real Estate Board of New York.

In my initial sales and marketing training, we were taught a couple of mantras that would help us to keep a positive mental attitude at all times while working with prospective home seekers during the sales presentation.

"Showtime" was one. This was used when an agent had a customer in the waiting area, and perhaps that agent had been dealing with a negative situation in the other room. Prior to greeting the customer, the sales team would do a one, two, shuffle, ball change, and say, "Showtime," and in no time the agent was greeting the prospect with a smile on her face and a change of attitude.

Now, who *really* loves cold-calling and phone work all day? You can tell the difference if someone to whom you are speaking on the phone has a negative attitude or a positive one. To keep a smile in your salespeople's voices when it may be time for the seventh-inning stretch, use phone aerobics. For example:

One, two
And you dial and dial
And smile and smile.

And you dial and dial
And smile and smile.

Putting a positive spin on every step to close the deal is the best advice I ever received.

THREE STEPS TO HAPPY CLIENTS

STEPHEN SHAPIRO

Stephen Shapiro is co-owner of Westside Estate Agency,
a real estate brokerage firm that sells homes on the west
side of Los Angeles and boasts the highest per-deal average
sale of any company in the nation.

I have been fortunate to work with some of the most influential business executives and monied individuals in the world. Part of my success has come from absorbing what I have heard from these people.

1. *Call back quickly*. One of the most important lessons I learned and have practiced for many years was taught to me by Kirk Kerkorian. Mr. Kerkorian personally called me on the phone; he did not have a secretary advancing him. Mr. Kerkorian on our real estate hunts impressed upon me how important it is to get back to your clients within an hour of their contact. Either call them back or have your secretary call them and say that Mr. Shapiro will call at a certain time if they will be there. The client then knows

that you are on top of the situation and are paying proper attention.

2. *Concentrate on the client.* The next key lesson is to recognize that as a real estate agent, you are in the service business. You work for the client, and your success is completely dependent on satisfying that client. So you as the agent must realize that you are never more important than the client, no matter what degree of success you have achieved.

3. *Protect your buyer.* I have learned that when you are representing a buyer, it is critical to impress on the buyer that it is always easier to get out of a deal than to lose a property you love to another buyer. When you let a buyer lose a deal to another, the client always blames the agent for not getting the deal for him or her.

SEVEN STEPS TO SUCCESS

MICHAEL SHVO

Michael Shvo, who has been named "the most successful
young real-estate broker in New York" by *New York* magazine,
is founder of the Shvo Group, whose listings include
New York's top luxury properties.

1. *Control greed.* Greed and real estate are two things that
go together. There's a lot of money to be made, and as somebody who markets and sells developments, I always have to
control other people's greed. The best advice I've gotten in
that sense is not to always try to take the last penny off the
table; make sure that the people who buy from you also
make money. If not, they won't buy from you again.

2. *Develop a unique product.* On the marketing side—this
is not advice that I've received but advice that I've given—
don't ever swim with the current. Try to go against it. If
you're developing a unique and different project—let's say
a Trump building—that building always will sell faster and
better than anything else. If you're building what every-

body else is building, once there's enough product on the market, all you're going to have to compete on is price. You never want to be the one competing on price. You always want to compete on product.

3. *Consider product and price.* Everybody will tell you that it's all about the location, but it's not only about the location. It's also the way you build at the location. People say location, location, location, but I would say location, product, price.

4. *Do not oversell.* Once somebody tells you that he wants to buy an apartment, once somebody tells you that you have the deal, stop talking about it. Talk about anything else. Talk about the weather. Talk about where you went to dinner last night. Most people will kill their own transaction by talking too much.

5. *Close before holiday weekends.* More deals die over a holiday weekend than at any other time. Over Thanksgiving or Christmas, for instance, if you have a deal that hasn't been signed or solidified before the holiday weekend, you probably have a 50 percent chance of losing that deal. People go home and see their family, and they say, "Well, I'm buying this building," or "I'm buying this apartment," and somebody always says, "Are you crazy? You're paying too much." It always happens. So you never want to have a deal open, an unsolidified deal, or a deal that's not signed before a holiday weekend.

6. *Consider changes.* One thing I've always believed is that just because everybody does something one way doesn't mean that it's the right way to do it. Every industry evolves, but the real estate business has not evolved in twenty or thirty years, especially on the marketing side. Everybody opens a sales office and prints a brochure with a floor plan; it all looks the same.

7. *Stand out.* I got a funny piece of advice from Donald. My last name is Shvo, and when I opened my company, I saw him that week, and he asked me what I named the company. I said "Shvo." And he said, "You have the most difficult name to pronounce, but you know what? Everybody is going to remember it."

PROCEED WITH PASSION—AND INTEGRITY!

LARRY SILVERSTEIN

Larry Silverstein is president and CEO of Silverstein Properties, Inc., which controls the World Trade Center site and is planning the rebuilding of its commercial space. He is founder and chairman emeritus of the New York University Real Estate Institute.

Whatever you do in life deserves to be done with your whole heart, to the best of your ability, and with a genuine passion to bring it to realization. Absolute integrity is the benchmark by which you must guide yourself in all of your endeavors.

Your reputation is your most precious possession. You must earn it; it cannot be bought. Your reputation takes a lifetime to build, but one foolish act can destroy it. As my father once counseled, "If you can't put something in bold type on the front page of the *New York Times* because it might embarrass you, don't do it!"

When dealing with people, treat them no differently than the way you want them to treat you.

TAKE A PROFIT AND MOVE ON

RAND SPERRY

Rand Sperry is CEO of Sperry Van Ness Equities
and Asset Management, which owns and manages retail,
office, and industrial space in Southern California.
He also cofounded the Sperry Van Ness commercial
and investment real estate brokerage firm.

You can't go broke taking a profit.

The meaning behind this advice is that so often we (principals) buy a building at the right price and the right timing. The price goes up, up, and away. The offers start coming in well beyond our expectations, yet we keep saying, "No." We become so greedy that we chase the market all the way up, and then the market starts to drop, and we chase it all the way down. Obviously the minute the market starts its downward spiral (and at some point it will), it's too late! By the time we sell the property, it is worth less than we paid. So, my point is, once you have achieved the profit growth you were projecting from the beginning, *take* your profit and run. Don't look back; move on to your next deal. Take your profit when the opportunity arises, or you may end up broke waiting for the big payoff.

KNOW YOUR MARKETPLACE

NORMAN STURNER

Norman Sturner is principal of Murray Hill Properties.

What's the best real estate advice I ever received? Before I tell you that secret, let me tell the story that led up to this best advice.

Sixteen years ago, we were offered a very good price to purchase a hotel on the grounds of the Denver Airport. We were aware of the adage "When something appears too good to be true, it probably is." Nevertheless, we did not want to pass up a bargain, and so out to Denver we went.

We hired architects, engineers, and consultants, and for three days we conducted our due diligence in order to ascertain why we New Yorkers were so fortunate to be offered this fine hotel out West at such a great price. After we looked into every nook and cranny, it indeed appeared to us that we had found a real bargain in a hotel in good repair with very favorable economics. The hotel had 95 percent occupancy twelve months a year.

My partner and I were congratulating ourselves with a toast at the hotel bar while we awaited our plane to take us home to begin the acquisition negotiations. The bartender approached and asked if we were the folks from New York City who were buying the hotel. We acknowledged that we were, whereupon he asked what we intended to do with the hotel when the new Denver airport was moved to Stapleton the following year.

It took just a moment for us to realize the reason for the bargain price. We thanked the bartender and left him a generous tip without acknowledging our lack of knowledge. Then we boarded the plane to take us home.

The best advice we have ever received and kept for the past thirty-five years is this: "Know your marketplace before you invest."

WORK HARD AND FOLLOW THROUGH

84

ROBERT E. SULENTIC

Robert E. Sulentic is chairman and
CEO of Trammell Crow Company.

Work hard, do what you say you're going to do, and remember that the people you interface with in the industry tend to come back around. This is a compilation of repeated advice I got from two or three people when I started with Trammell Crow Company.

Work Hard

Experience has shown that if you're working a deal with an investor or client, it's very important to put a plan in place and work hard to execute that plan. If things don't turn out but you've worked hard according to your plan, the other party will be more likely to give you a second chance. More important, if things do turn out well, the result is extremely powerful.

Do What You Say

I learned the importance of this when I worked in one of our local offices and our team routinely set business priorities. We were careful about picking the right objectives and were committed to hitting the objectives we stated. That focus gave us the discipline to stay on course with the things that mattered most. In fact, staying focused and on course is the only way it really works—otherwise you waste time and energy with abandoned efforts that end up having no payback, and you get no benefit from all your hard work.

People Tend to Come Back Around

Over the years, we have had many reminders that it is always a good idea to maintain positive relationships with the people we encounter in the industry. For example, former Trammell Crow Company associates showed up later as clients; customers from one company, who then went to another company, chose to hire us again; and even people formerly with our competitors ended up working for our company.

COMMIT YOURSELF TO WINNING

STEFAN SWANEPOEL

Stefan Swanepoel is chairman and CEO of RealtyU® Group, Inc.,
the largest career development company in the country,
educating more than 400,000 real estate professionals
annually, and author of *Real Estate Confronts Reality*
and its sequel, *Real Estate Confronts the Future.*

My father once said, "Business is like chess. The chess-board is the world and all your options; the chess pieces represent society and the people; the rules of chess are like the laws of doing business; and your competitor represents the challenges you must overcome to achieve your goals."

If you are a weak player in any sport, you are usually no match for a professional player. Chess, business, and real estate are no exceptions, and yet in business almost everyone thinks he or she is better than the professionals. Being the best, whether in sports or business, requires far more commitment than just showing up to play. It involves acquiring skills, ones that are practiced and improved over time.

For example, if you are an average chess player, you may be thinking about your current move and maybe even the next move or two. However, a chess champion would be planning five, six, or seven moves ahead, thinking through alternate situations, visualizing possible locations for the various pieces, anticipating your possible moves and his response before you have even made your move.

DON'T COUNT ON LUCK

Of course, luck can and sometimes does turn the tide in your favor, and it has created its share of millionaires in real estate, sometimes even in spite of themselves. But that isn't the norm. The hard truth is that success is the result of solid thinking, the evaluation of options, the anticipation, identification, and quantifying of hurdles, the development and organization of priorities, the creation of strategies, and the decisiveness of execution.

HAVE A SOUND STRATEGY

In real estate as in chess, it's all about strategy, and strategy requires planning. You must consciously think about your plan. A sound strategy helps coordinate your moves, your actions, your defenses, and your attack. And just one plan is not enough. You need multiple plans with at least another one or two contingency plans.

In business, real estate, and life, good planning saves money, time, and effort and provides you the best odds for a good result. The long-term outcome of a well-thought-out and well-conceptualized business plan is a progressive, positive advancement regardless of the business climate. A failure in good planning often creates bad results.

PRIORITIZE TASKS

An absolute must in planning is to begin by breaking larger events and tasks into smaller ones. Then identify and prioritize between the urgent and the important tasks—between events of higher and lower concern. Only then are you ready to decide what pieces to move, when, and where.

In chess, the game isn't over until you secure a checkmate or your opponent quits—neither of which is likely to occur unless you constantly manage and revise your plan. Things can change dramatically in a single move, and winning—especially against a fierce competitor—requires constant situational analysis and the skillful execution of required plan changes.

KNOW THE RULES OF THE GAME

Almost everyone would agree that you can't win a game if you don't know the rules. Real estate has more than its fair share of both rules and nuances, and it is an extremely complex industry. For the average person, a real estate transaction represents the most expensive and complicated financial deal in his lifetime. The stakes are high, and one cannot afford to weigh in without understanding all the options.

ANALYZE STRENGTHS AND WEAKNESSES

If your real estate business is not enjoying the success you planned, your only option is to step back and analyze it—*find out why*. If your business is enjoying great success, also step back and analyze it and *find out why*.

Examine your company's strengths and weaknesses. Review your vision and focus. Assess your objectives, and confirm the results you want to achieve. Then, and only then, perform a reality check, and make the necessary adjustments. You must also know your team members. You must have an intimate understanding of their skills and attributes in order to utilize all the members of your team to their fullest potential.

In short, maximize what you have.

KEEP A STEP AHEAD

When chess is played by a champion, the possibility of chance is practically eliminated. Chess is all about strategy, tactics, concentration, and execution. To be successful, you don't have to know all the moves or the answers. You just need to remain a step or two ahead of your opponent. In the real estate business also, you need to stay a move or two ahead of the rest of the market.

STAY ON TRACK

Great plans fail because people fail to focus on and execute their plans. They frequently become distracted, hesitate, lose focus or interest, or just plain forget. It is not good positioning that wins games. Rather, it is good moves being executed correctly and appropriately.

Success requires staying on track and pushing forward with determination, tenacity, and persistence. Keep your eyes on the long-term objective as well as on the immediate priorities. Skillful execution is delivering the winning move when you need it the most. Without constant evaluation and reevaluation of the circumstances surrounding the game, the brief opportunity to deliver that move may slip by unnoticed in the midst of confusion and chaos.

In both the world of chess and the world of real estate, it's all about planning, commitment, and execution.

DON'T JUDGE A BOOK BY ITS COVER

EMILY TANNEN

Emily Tannen is director of sales and marketing and corporate vice president of A. J. Clarke Real Estate Corporation and a member of the Real Estate Board of New York.

In the 1960s, the founder of my company, Alexander J. Clarke, and his teenage son were working in the garden on their estate in New Jersey. A. J. glanced over at the garage and noticed that the Cadillac had seen better days. "C'mon, son, let's go," he said. Still dressed in their gardening clothes, they drove to the nearest Cadillac dealer. No one gave them the time of day. After a while of just hanging around the showroom, father and son left and drove to the dealership in the next town. There, a salesman greeted them with "Good afternoon, gentlemen. How can I help you?" That salesman sold them a brand-new Cadillac for cash.

Clearly the moral is that you can't judge a book by its cover. I've seen it again and again through the years. The customer in the Armani who simply reeks of money doesn't

233

TRUMP

have two nickels, and the one you think couldn't buy dinner ends up being the megamillionaire. It's absolutely impossible for the broker to guess who's real and who's not by how the person looks or presents himself. Therefore, it's imperative for the real estate professional to treat all clients and potential clients with the same respect. Some deals will get made and some won't, but the broker can't lose.

CHOOSE WHERE YOU WANT TO LIVE

Location, location, location. Gosh, who first came up with that? But you know, it's the truth. First, choose where you want to live. Everything else is secondary. In 1998, my husband and I were looking to rent a weekend home in Woodstock. We saw lots of houses in varying price ranges. Some were quite lovely, spacious, beautifully designed. Our target price kept inching upward. Nothing, however, really grabbed us, and we weren't sure why. Eventually we were taken by our broker to a house on a mountainside, on a very private road on the north side of the mountain facing south, with sun and views that seemed to go on forever. My husband stepped out on the deck, looked at the view, then turned to the broker and asked, "Is this house for sale?" On the way home, he asked me how many bedrooms and bathrooms the house had. It really didn't matter because he had fallen in love with the location. Of course, we bought the house.

234

WHEN IN DOUBT, BUY

The best real estate advice I ever had was "buy." When in doubt, buy.

But don't speculate unless you are dead sure that the trend is up, up, and up. In a market that is going down or even iffy, speculators can get hurt. For example, if someone buys at a preconstruction price expecting to sell at market price when the property is built, and in the interim, the market goes down, the speculator may have to sell at a loss. If the speculator needs to put up more money than she has or than the bank will lend her, she will lose money. If the market goes down and she has to sell for any reason, she may lose money.

But the buyer who is purchasing for his own use will almost always come out the winner. If he sells in a down market, he will get less; however, the trade-up property will cost less, so it's a wash. If he sells in an up market, he'll get more; however, what he's buying with the proceeds will cost proportionately more as well. There's no downside. You absolutely can't lose.

The lesson is: buy it. If you don't have enough money, borrow it. Don't let the opportunity pass. Just do it. You'll never be sorry.

THREE LESSONS FROM MY FATHER

ROBERT S. TAUBMAN

Robert S. Taubman is chairman, president, and
CEO of Taubman Centers, Inc., a leading developer
and manager of major retail properties. Taubman has headed
Taubman Centers, a real estate investment trust, since
its pioneering public offering in 1992.

Growing up in a real estate family, I got plenty of advice—solicited and otherwise—from my father, Alfred Taubman. While I could fill a book with his wisdom, three lessons have been particularly important to me.

First, forget about the old adage that the three most important things in real estate are location, location, location. In retail real estate in particular, you make your own location. Sure, having an accessible site at the heart of an affluent region is significant. But a shopping center location becomes dominant in its market by virtue of its anchor tenants, merchandise mix, design, management, and marketing. In the mall business, where you are becomes secondary to what and who you are—and how you stay fresh and relevant to your customer over time.

Second, understand that a powerful force we call *threshold resistance* is always standing between you and your customer. Everything we do in developing and operating our shopping centers is designed to break down the barriers and inconveniences that keep shoppers from coming on a regular basis to our properties and ultimately crossing over the thresholds of our stores. There are a thousand reasons customers will go someplace other than your property. You have to give them at least a thousand and one reasons to come to you.

Third, never get bored with your business. A successful real estate developer's energy, passion, and skill are not automatically transferable to other fields and endeavors—even if he thinks so! Sticking to your knitting—and what you know—will keep you out of trouble and assure that your real estate business gets the attention and resources it deserves. Besides, real estate got you rich, and when done correctly, it should never be boring.

TRUST, TIMING, TERMS, AND TRUTH

JOSEPH THANHAUSER

Joseph Thanhauser is chairman of Byrnam Wood, LLC,
a global real estate services firm, and a fellow of
The Royal Institution of Chartered Surveyors.

I negotiate leases for tenants anywhere in the world, but the advice I've received is applicable in all markets. That advice has come to me over more than thirty years, and several memorable bits of the best advice I've received follow here.

BUILD TRUST

One of our longtime clients, Michael Moore of the DMB&B advertising agency, once explained quite concisely why he liked my approach: "Clients want to be intelligently, professionally, and aggressively represented, but most of all they want to be *fiercely* represented." He was telling me that he assumed I would negotiate hard on his behalf, but more than that, he was saying that he trusted me to always place his interest above my own. Routinely one signature on a lease can mean millions of dollars to a broker or adviser, and a level of trust is either there or it isn't. In such situations, a person can be objective, but it is difficult to be impartial. Mike made it clear that I always had been—and must always be—impartial where my own interest is concerned, and fiercely partisan on behalf of my clients' interests from start to finish.

MAKE A DEAL—NOW

At the beginning of my career, working for a large New York developer, I was told that the Uris brothers who founded the company had a simple philosophy: do the first sensible deal that comes along. I didn't fully comprehend the neat practicality of the idea until I had experienced both parts of the market cycle. In high, landlord-oriented markets, it's not unusual for several tenants to pursue the same space; in low, tenant-oriented markets, tenants have more options to choose from and frequently negotiate for several options simultaneously. These extreme ends of any market cycle sorely test the ethics of most landlords and tenants, but during the majority of the cycle, the advice to make the first deal that is doable at sensible terms ensures the integrity of the process and the relationship that develops from it.

SET REASONABLE TERMS

Time and again I have seen deals fall apart because they are at terms that one side or the other simply can't afford.

Or worse: when such deals do get done and reality sets in, either the tenant is burdened with an unaffordable lease obligation, or the landlord has given away too much and gets in trouble (which cannot mean good things for the tenant). Whenever I see such situations, I think back to the advice I received from Howard Sonn thirty years ago: "Too sharp won't cut." Unlike most places on earth, the commercial property markets in the U.S. are pretty much pure, unfettered capitalism, and the position of advantage shifts—sometimes vehemently—from one side to the other. To negotiate without a feel for what the other side needs to survive is to risk, or even to ensure, that the resulting deal will not be doable, or will lead to much unhappiness.

MEET TROUBLESOME ISSUES HEAD-ON

In one of his first post-administration books, Henry Kissinger observed that whatever must ultimately be done should be done immediately. That little nugget had a lasting impact on me because real estate is a field that is very competitive and hardly free from conflict. While we have had very few contentious situations over the years, it is possible for men of goodwill to disagree almost to the point of bloodshed. Usually these have been situations where, had we but joined the issues up front instead of phumphing and putting them aside, we could have saved a lot of time, money, and aggravation. I regard my word as my bond, but not everyone acts that way, and when we have let issues slide—particularly of compensation, of percentage, of division of labor—they have frequently come back to whack us on the head.

Recognize the Eternal Verity

The four most expensive words in the English language: *this time it's different.* With the perspective of several market cycles, it's clear to me that it is arrogant and stupid to predicate any deal or negotiation on the perpetual increase or decline of things. I have seen my share of buyers who have denied the fundamental nature of the real estate market. It wasn't so long ago that we heard the cost of real estate in Japan was so high that the value of the Japanese Imperial Palace and grounds was worth more than the state of California. Ultimately the law of gravity had not been repealed; values fell, and the seasons continued in progression. It wasn't different.

The cyclical nature of real estate in major commercial markets is as immutable as the seasons. Perhaps it is the nature of real estate—involving long-term commitments by people who base their judgments on current trends and immediate resources—that stimulates the human tendency to extrapolate to the horizon and beyond. Perhaps it is the enormous, complex array of resources that must be brought to bear in large projects that virtually demands such extrapolation. Perhaps, when rents are falling, supply is rising, and projects are failing, the temptation to project such trends to an extreme is almost irresistible. In any event, while nobody can foretell the future, it is just as important to bear in mind that the future is not necessarily a linear extrapolation of the present. Write that advice in large letters.

RECOGNIZE THE GEOGRAPHIC VERITY

It's different here (the geographic equivalent of the eternal verity). Frequently when we go to markets in foreign countries, or even places as exotic as Chicago or Detroit, we hear this old refrain. In fact, the principal similarities we have experienced throughout the world are that (1) people everywhere tell us, "It's different here. Why don't you just turn around and go home?"; and (2) if we are sensitive to the local interpretation of space, rent, term, and the other usual fundamentals, we can generally negotiate terms superior to market and get out of town before the "Wanted" posters are up. Tsubos, meters, pings, hectares . . . in short, it isn't different, here or anywhere. Sunlight and gravity are pretty much the same everywhere, and the fundamentals we have learned in the open markets throughout the U.S. apply broadly throughout the world.

That said, there are local nuances and customs in every market that can be very useful or very harmful, and it is essential to be aware of them. We frequently tell clients that smart people might get 98 percent of what we could negotiate, but would die in the last 2 percent. In unfamiliar markets, to avoid this fate, it's usually easier to make judgments about the intelligence, integrity, and reliability of a local colleague who can give us the insights we need than to try to master the subtleties of each market.

DEVELOPING A SUCCESSFUL
HOMEOWNER ASSOCIATION

RICHARD THOMPSON

Richard Thompson is the owner of Regenesis, a management consulting company specializing in condominium and homeowner associations. He is nationally recognized as the HOA Expert and has written numerous articles on homeowner associations.

Lifestyles of the twenty-first century have radically changed from those of fifty years ago. The clamor for big lots and single-family houses has been replaced by a demand for condominiums and planned communities (generically called "homeowner associations," or HOAs).

The growth of HOAs has been nothing short of *phenomenal* in the last decade. In many urban areas, as much as 75 percent of all new residential housing is in the form of a homeowner association. Mixed-use HOAs combine residential and commercial. For instance, retail and office units often occupy street-level space in a building while residential units occupy upper floors.

HOAs are essentially governmental corporations controlled by the members through an elected board of directors. The HOA has the authority to make and enforce rules and regulations and to collect fees from the members to support the HOA's operation and maintenance responsibilities. Like the IRS, the HOA has significant power to enforce its will through liens and, in extreme cases, foreclosure.

When homeowner associations are properly conceived and constructed, they work very well. When they are haphazardly implemented, trouble and discontent follow. The success or failure of an HOA begins at the beginning with the developer.

Knowing the huge potential in HOA development, what should the savvy HOA developer do to maximize sales and profits? I will explain several steps to being a successful homeowner association developer.

1. *Choose the HOA's design and materials carefully.* Homeowner associations often have significant maintenance, repair, and replacement responsibilities. This is particularly true of condominiums where the maintenance of the structures and grounds is the responsibility of the HOA. This responsibility falls on the shoulders of a volunteer board of directors, which is usually composed of well-meaning but inexperienced people. So, when it comes to designing the structure and grounds, ease of maintenance and cost of repairs are extremely important.

Steer clear of unproven designs and materials with little or no warranty. The odds are high that such an experiment will fail and problems will come back to haunt the developer. The more complex and expensive it is for the HOA to be maintained, the more likely it is that such maintenance will not be done properly.

2. *Carefully craft the governing documents.* Also called CC&Rs (covenants, conditions, and restrictions), the rules, regulations, declarations, and bylaws in these documents form the HOA governmental structure. State laws vary on the requirements, and so it is imperative that these documents be crafted by an experienced attorney in the state where the development is going to be. There is no such thing as "boilerplate" governing documents. Each HOA is unique, and state laws change frequently. Never try to save money on legal costs, because poorly written governing documents can make it next to impossible for the board to administer HOA business, enforce reasonable rules, or raise the money needed to maintain the assets.

3. *Budget the HOA adequately.* In an attempt to be competitive in selling their HOA units, some developers set the HOA fees unrealistically low. If the competition is charging $300 a month, they might charge $250. That's a better deal, right? Hardly. If it takes $300 a month per unit to support the HOA budget, it won't take long for the new board of directors to figure that out, and then Mr. Developer

receives a strongly worded letter from an attorney that has ugly words like *misrepresentation* and *fraud* sprinkled here and there. Whether the developer has intentionally or unintentionally underestimated the HOA budget, he will be held accountable. Moreover, if the HOA doesn't have enough money to maintain the assets, it will fail sooner, and the developer usually gets blamed for construction defects.

It's best to use third-party consultants, including professional HOA managers, CPAs, and management consultants that specialize in homeowner associations to determine the HOA's operating and reserve budgets. The developer should get as arm's length as possible from the HOA budget numbers.

4. *Provide a reserve study.* A reserve study forecasts the repair and replacement events that the HOA will encounter over the next thirty years. It identifies the common elements by component (roof, paint, siding, etc.), assigns a repair or replacement cost to each, a schedule for each (e.g., roof, thirty years; paint, ten years), and a funding plan that guides the board of directors on how much money to reserve each year for these future events. Since these costs can easily add up to millions of dollars, it's critical that they be included in the HOA budget from the beginning. Then, it's a relatively simple matter to collect the money each month from each owner, deposit it into a reserve account,

and spend it on the indicated repairs and replacements as they happen. The HOAs that follow such a plan are well maintained, the owners enjoy high resale value, and the community is livable and desirable.

5. *Provide a maintenance plan.* While adequate budgets can pay for adequate maintenance, *how* the money is spent is very important. Remember, the board is made up of amateurs who often don't have the knowledge or experience to maintain the millions of dollars in assets with which they are entrusted. A maintenance plan written by the developer gets into the specifics of what should be done, who should do it, and when. The plan should be written in layman's terms because that's what the board members are. They need to understand what needs to be done, but they will not actually do it themselves. A maintenance plan that ties directly to the operating budget and reserve study will give the board the guidance it needs to spend the HOA's money properly.

6. *Honor warranty obligations.* Developers generally have a statutory warranty period on HOA property sold. Handling warranty claims properly and quickly yields big dividends in the public relations department. It's best to have someone specifically assigned to this task since it takes a high degree of organization that average contractors don't have. Besides being the right thing to do, honoring warranty obligations produces goodwill that will be invalu-

able in the future dealings that may be confrontational. A happy history eases future fights.

7. *Stay in the mix.* Just because the project is sold out and turned over to the homeowners doesn't mean the developer's job is over. Beyond warranty issues, there is always a potential that some legal claim may raise its ugly head. To help fend off these dragons, the developer should retain the right in the governing documents to attend future board meetings and receive copies of board meeting minutes. Proactive developers take those rights seriously and attend all meetings for *years.* The result is that small problems are nipped in the bud before they become subjects of litigation.

Being an HOA developer can be highly rewarding and profitable when the plan includes these insider principles. Take this advice to heart and enjoy hearty results.

FIT BUILDINGS TO THE COMMUNITY

JONATHAN M. TISCH

Jonathan M. Tisch is chairman and CEO of Loews Hotels and author of *The Power of We: Succeeding Through Partnerships.*

As chairman of Loews Hotels, I spend most of my time in the world of real estate intersecting with the world of hospitality. Hotels are unlike most other businesses; we are open 24 hours a day, 7 days a week, and 365 days a year. If a hotel is not successful, we can't just pick up and move to another location. So it's incumbent on us to become part of the community.

One way we do that is by making our hotels fit the local environment through the use of architecture and interior design. Our insistence on developing properties that complement their surroundings is part of our practice of treating the communities we serve not merely as customers, but as partners. One beautiful example is in Miami Beach.

In 1993, before the resurgence of South Beach, the city announced a competition to pick a partner to build a new, luxury hotel to help revive the local economy, support the nearby convention center, and spur economic development. It would be the first major hotel to be constructed there in thirty years, and every major hotel company in America responded to the request for proposals, touching off an intense bidding process.

We crafted an impressive package and worked hard to make the best possible use of the proposed location for the hotel—a five-acre site at Collins Avenue and Sixteenth Street in the heart of Miami Beach's historic Art Deco district. It included the historic St. Moritz Hotel, a long-disused property dating to 1927 that the winning firm would be expected to renovate and include in the new facility. Our plans called for a hotel on a grand scale that would harmonize with rather than fight the magnificent artistic heritage of the neighborhood.

After the plans were presented, the Loews design quickly won praise. The *Miami Herald* architecture critic, Peter Whoriskey, observed that our plan "actually fit" the challenging beachfront site and that we succeeded "by respecting the peculiar urban/beach blend of the neighborhood."

Soon after the announcement that Loews had won the bid, future bookings at the Miami Beach Convention Center jumped by 289 percent. We restored the St. Moritz to its original Art Deco splendor and constructed our new hotel tower on the adjacent property.

To be successful in real estate, you need to be not just part of the community but also reflective of the community. The Loews Miami Beach Hotel, with its iconic Art Deco spire, became an instant landmark when it opened on December 24, 1998. It helped revitalize a formerly depressed neighborhood and transformed Collins Avenue into one of the most prestigious hotel corridors in the world today.

GROW STRATEGICALLY

MARJORIE TORRES

Marjorie Torres is founder and CEO of Concrete Stories,
a commercial real estate advisory firm that provides landlords,
tenants, and investors with strategic advice, brokerage,
negotiation, and real estate development services.

As a Latina serial entrepreneur, I have had the privilege of
receiving phenomenal advice from extraordinary world-class executives. Their global experience has allowed me to
keep a competitive edge in every area I have decided to enter.

I started my firm, Concrete Stories, by focusing on
reengineering the leasing and sales brokerage process of
commercial real estate. As I have been exposed to commercial real estate opportunities throughout the world, my
background in industrial engineering and investment banking has helped me determine whether a particular project
was worth pursuing.

Maintain Majority Control

The most important advice I received at first was that in order for my firm to maintain my vision, I needed to have majority control of the company. I raised venture capital for my firm, and we now have institutional investors such as Credit Suisse First Boston Merchant Capital, Columbia University, and Wesleyan University. It took very arduous negotiations, but I followed the advice and still control the firm and own more than 70 percent of the equity.

Differentiate Your Firm From Competitors

At the next stage of growth, the best advice I received was that I needed to differentiate myself from the competition and focus on a rich niche to mine. As a result, we started providing strategic real estate advice for companies that held real estate in their portfolios. We targeted private equity firms and institutional investors. Representatives of these firms sit on boards and control portfolios of companies that need real estate services. These firms learned the lessons of the dot-com era. Our firm comes in as their out-sourced facilities group. We help the portfolio company CEOs solve their expansion and contraction issues.

Think Big

More recently, the best advice I received was that I needed to think big! I had all the assets I needed to compete, and it was time to take the plunge into development. We understand the New York City market, and we were providing cost-effective development strategies for our clients. Now, as principals, we are developing various projects from 50,000 square feet to more than 1 million square feet.

ALWAYS REMEMBER TO LISTEN

In all of these stages of growth, I never forgot the simple key: real estate is a people business; learn to listen. We are alchemists. We have to decipher the currency of exchange of each party: the community effect (social capital), jobs creation (political capital), rates of return (economic capital), and more. Our firm successfully transforms one currency into another and helps build great projects. Creating win-win situations makes deals happen.

THERE IS NO SUBSTITUTE FOR PASSION

DONALD TRUMP JR.

Donald Trump Jr. is executive vice president of development and acquisitions for The Trump Organization.

The best advice I have ever received is, "There is no substitute for passion."

The most successful leaders inspire the people around them by motivating them with their passion and instincts. So whether it is a real estate deal or any other venture, the key is to find something you enjoy doing, and then do it better than anyone else—because success comes easier to people who follow their passion.

BUILD YOUR REPUTATION CAREFULLY

IVANKA M. TRUMP

Ivanka M. Trump joined The Trump Organization in 2005
as a member of the development team. She actively participates
in all aspects of real estate development from deal evaluation,
analysis and predevelopment planning to construction,
marketing, operations, sales, and leasing.

As a young person in business, it is extremely important to create a great track record. You need to set your own standard and you need to be consistent and true to your word. Your dedication should be at its maximum. Your actions should be flawlessly executed. Start building your reputation from the very beginning. Take your reputation seriously as it is one of the most essential elements you can exert control over.

HAVE FUN AS YOU'RE PROFITING

94

STEVE VAN AMBURGH

Steve Van Amburgh is CEO of Koll Development Company,
one of the nation's leading commercial real estate firms.

When you and your company have confidence, you can
have lots of fun. Everyone likes to have fun.

And it seems that when you are having lots of fun, you
exceed everyone's expectations, win lots of new projects,
and achieve amazing results. Have fun and win. That's the
best advice we can give anyone in our business seeking
advice.

FOCUS ON QUALITY

95

LEO F. WELLS III

Leo F. Wells is founder and president of
Wells Real Estate Funds, Inc., whose affiliated real estate
investment trusts and other investment vehicles serve more
than 200,000 investors, specializing in class A office
properties and other real estate opportunities.

Sometimes advice comes in the form of a joke. There's an old one in real estate and investing circles, which I heard years ago and still tell to this day.

In the final days of World War II, a ship loaded with sardines is headed to Europe for the troops. While it's en route, the war ends, and the ship turns back to the harbor at New York. The shipper figures he'd better sell these fish—and fast.

Soon, he finds a buyer at a nickel a can and happily unloads the sardines. That buyer sells to another at 6 cents a can. That buyer finds another dealer to pay 7 cents . . . and so on up to 10 cents.

Finally a wholesaler pays 15 cents a can and sells the sardines to a grocery store for 20 cents. The sardines then go on the shelf at 25 cents a can.

Soon, angry customers return to the store. The sardines are rotten. The store manager calls his wholesaler.

"My customers are furious—why'd you sell me rotten sardines?" he asks.

"Those sardines weren't for eating," comes the reply. "They're for trading."

When the real estate market is percolating, there may be big money to be had in trading—but eventually someone has to make use of the property, and its true value will be apparent. At some point, somebody has to eat the sardines. And at that point investors in quality real estate can prosper, while others wind up with a real stink on their hands.

In real estate, as in so many areas in business, it's quality that matters. I've found that focusing on that—quality properties, quality service, quality tenants—can spell success in the long run.

KNOW YOUR EXIT STRATEGY
BEFORE BUYING

BRETT WHITE

Brett White is president and CEO of CB Richard Ellis.

During the early 1990s and again in 2001 and 2002, real estate fundamentals declined for a variety of reasons. Because of this, many prognosticators declared commercial real estate to be dead or at least significantly out of favor. Contrary to these views, a number of the smartest investors in the business bought as much commercial real estate as they could lay their hands on. Of course, these investors were richly rewarded for their foresight. The lesson here is that in the long run, commercial real estate is a very resilient asset class, and history has shown that if one has the wherewithal to buy commercial real estate when others in the market feel it is out of favor, those investments will pay off handsomely.

Friends and customers often ask me to tell them whether buying a certain piece of commercial real estate is a wise decision. Is it priced too high? Should they wait for a decline in price before buying? These and many other questions cause them to hesitate before making the purchase.

I've always answered these people by reminding them that their decision should be driven by their exit strategy. If you are purchasing a piece of commercial real estate as part of your long-term portfolio and want to hold on to it as an investment, then the one thing I can tell you for certain is that in the long run, real estate appreciates in value regardless of economic cycles, new technologies, global competition, or any other external factor. There are very few people who can say they lost money on commercial real estate if they held it for fifteen to twenty years or more. This is one of the terrific aspects about commercial real estate.

DEAL WHEN YOU NEED TO DEAL

KEN WILSON

Ken Wilson is cofounder and CEO of
Capital Hotel Management, LLC.

After twenty-five years in hotel real estate investment, I have learned many lessons about what it takes to be successful. My recipe for success requires the following:

Vision. Don't let the deal define you; instead define each deal by what you can do with it. Any good real estate deal requires vision as well as the capital and experienced and committed professional staff to convert that vision into reality.

Timing. Timing is everything. Know when to get in and when to get out. It is better to be 80 percent right than 100 percent wrong.

Risk. Never risk too much at any one time or on any one deal. In real estate deals, particularly hotels, so much lies out of your control. One event can change a good deal to a bad one overnight. Remember, risk and reward are directly related.

Close. Don't let a good deal die on the table—you never know how good the deal really was until you close it. And you can usually tell a good deal when both the buyer and the seller leave the closing room equally satisfied.

WALK AWAY IF NECESSARY

SCOTT A. WOLSTEIN

Scott A. Wolstein is chairman and CEO of Developers Diversified Realty, a real estate investment trust that manages properties in forty-four states and Puerto Rico.

My father, Bart Wolstein, gave me the most important real estate advice I ever received: "Be prepared to close your briefcase and walk away." It was simple advice, but it has come into play time and again. When you enter a real estate negotiation, you must know your point of indifference, the point at which you feel equally good or bad if the deal proceeds or not. When that point is crossed, you need to be prepared to close your briefcase and walk out of the room. If you are not prepared to do that, you will make a bad deal.

Real estate entrepreneurs too often fall in love with deals. This can be a fatal error. There are lots of deals. Infatuation with any one opportunity is problematic. During a speech to a throng of real estate professionals, Albert Ratner, a friend in the industry, once quipped, "There should be a new twenty-four-hour hotline called Developers Anonymous. You call any time of day and explain your deal, and they talk you out of it!" Funny, but so true. Every real estate principal needs to have that "hotline" in the back of his mind when he approaches a negotiation.

Also, the most important skill to successful real estate negotiations is the ability to listen. In order to consummate a successful transaction, one needs to clearly understand the "hot buttons" for the person on the other side of the table. You already know what you want out of the deal. The art is learning what your adversary wants. Once you know what his needs are, you know what you need to do to structure the transaction to give you what you need and accommodate his needs as well. Often, it is not a zero-sum game. What is important to him may not be of any appreciable cost to you. Find out what that is, and you'll be well ahead of the game. Spend less time convincing your adversary to give you what you want, and spend more time listening to his needs and trying to accommodate them. If it doesn't work, close your briefcase and walk away!

FIVE RULES FOR SUCCESS
OF YOUR BUSINESS

ROB ZACHE

Rob Zache is president of Central Place Real Estate,
whose focus is hotel, restaurant, and commercial
real estate across the Midwest.

While I am strictly in commercial real estate, I will offer
two perspectives, one for residential and the other for
commercial.

RESIDENTIAL

When it comes to buying a home, my advice is "Buy
the neighborhood, not the house." This is basically back-
ward from the process of most home buyers.

Most residential buyers don't understand the many factors that affect the value of residential properties. They just
want to live in a house like the one in which they grew up,
and they proceed to buy a house like that, wherever it may
be located. That can be a fatal flaw. They may find a house

they like—except it is in a bad neighborhood—and may never get their equity out of the house when they sell it.

I suggest buying a home more for resale value than for emotional attachment. I've seen quite a few people buy a place they love, only to regret it when they take a financial bath at the sale of the house. These people bought the property emotionally in the first place rather than pragmatically understanding that location will drive up or detract from value. The neighborhood is one of the most important factors to consider in a home purchase.

My advice is to find the neighborhood you like best and then select the best home for you in the neighborhood. It may not be the perfect home, but it will be the best combination of factors you need to get the maximum value and not lose your shirt when you sell. Neighborhoods drive values more than the individual homes do. For example, the part of town (white collar vs. blue collar), the surroundings of the neighborhood (industrial zones, train tracks vs. parks, water, or class A office parks), the routes you must use to drive to and from the neighborhood (congested highways, industrial zones vs. tree-lined upscale commercial or residential areas), and the neighborhood itself (new vs. old, large vs. small houses, tract vs. architectural designs, trees vs. cornfield development) all affect neighborhood values.

Additionally, pick the best neighborhood you can afford. Then select a house in the lower or middle end of the price range in that neighborhood. The value and strength of the neighborhood will raise the value of the lower and middle price ranges faster than the upper price ranges. Never select a house in the upper price range. You will rarely get your money out if you pick the most expensive home in the area because it will always seem overpriced compared to the other houses around it.

COMMERCIAL

I've been in the commercial real estate, development, and brokerage business for twenty-five years and almost exclusively in the franchise industry, including being trained by and concluding many deals with companies like Hilton, Marriott, Promus, and Outback Steakhouse. I have been involved in more than one hundred major deals in eight states totaling over $1 billion in total project value.

The most important thing the franchise business has taught me is that if you follow a few simple rules, any business—I repeat, any business—will succeed.

It took me a while to realize that there are simply not a lot of people who can run successful businesses. Years ago the franchise industry picked up on this and developed a system of running a business that can be applied to most other businesses or situations. Most follow this program. And most succeed. That's why you see a lot of chain or franchise signs taking over business from the old mom-and-pop businesses that didn't know or didn't follow these simple rules. If they did, they'd succeed more often or at least be able to compete better.

My five rules of running a successful business are to get the following right: (1) the market; (2) the site; (3) the facility; (4) the product; and (5) the management. If you get those five rules right, you will succeed as well as you can possibly succeed.

1. *The market.* Make sure you are doing business in the right market, meaning the right city, and also the right submarket or neighborhood within that city. Don't try to open a hotel in the middle of nowhere with no population or traffic generators. Don't try to open a restaurant where the demographics or income won't support your concept. Don't open an upscale spa next to a blue-collar industrial town on the downswing, or try to sell snowballs in Alaska. Make sure your concept fits the market; analyze demographics, flyspeck competition, and get a good feel for demand. Match the market to the product. This sounds so obvious, but you would not believe how many businesses miss this simple rule.

2. *The site.* Once you have determined the market, find the best possible site in that market to fit your concept. And (within reason) pay whatever you have to in order to get the best piece of real estate for your business. One of the biggest mistakes I've seen is businesses underpaying for real

estate, thinking the business is good enough to make up for a secondary location. That's a big mistake. That decision will likely cause the failure of the business or at least the guarantee of a marginal business. Pay for the dirt. Get the best location. Real estate is location, location, location for a good reason. It will pay off in spades in the long term, but if you don't buy the best piece of real estate for your business, then you will be paying for it instead. Don't cheap out. Just do it and deal with it.

3. *The facility.* Build or buy the facility to make the business shine. Buildings are constructed for the operations of the business, not vice versa. The building should make the operation or business within it work seamlessly, efficiently, effectively. If it also has to be beautiful, make it beautiful. Design it to accomplish the operations at which the business needs to excel in order to do what the customer needs or expects. If the facility is not maximized for operations, then the business will never reach its potential; it will always have a roadblock in the way of maximum success.

4. *The product.* Get your product correct from the start, whether it is hard or soft goods retail, food in a restaurant, or service and a good night's sleep in a hotel. Know what your customer wants, what your product is, and make it part of your mission statement to provide the best product in the market that will satisfy your customer *every time.* Is it service, sales, a thing, or a combination? Know your cus-

tomers and what product they want. Present the product in a way the customers appreciate. But get the product right.

5. *The management.* Once the first four things are in place, they are in place more or less permanently, and after that, management takes over. Without good management, all the time, effort, and money to get to that point can be wasted. Management can take up another whole book, and it includes everything from customers to staffing to marketing, revenue generation, expense control, finance, and accounting. This is the true art of a long-term business and must be detailed and flyspecked daily, constantly. Continual improvement of management is necessary today to survive. Watch the pennies, and the dollars will follow.

BUY LOW, SELL HIGH, AND DON'T BE GREEDY

MORTIMER ZUCKERMAN

Mortimer Zuckerman is cofounder and chairman of
Boston Properties, Inc. He is also chairman and editor-in-
chief of *U.S. News & World Report* and chairman
and publisher of the *New York Daily News*.

B uy low, sell high, and don't be greedy.

TRUMP

The best real
estate advice I
ever received
**available in
Spanish**

ISBN: 0881130028

GRUPO NELSON
Una división de Thomas Nelson Publishers
Juntos inspiramos al mundo
www.gruponelson.com